Earth's Place in the Universe

elevate science
MODULES

SAVVAS
LEARNING COMPANY

You're an author!

As you write in this science book, your answers and personal discoveries will be recorded for you to keep, making this book unique to you. That is why you are one of the primary authors of this book.

✏️ **In the space below, print your name, school, town, and state. Then write a short autobiography that includes your interests and accomplishments.**

YOUR NAME ....

SCHOOL ....

TOWN, STATE ....

AUTOBIOGRAPHY ....

....

Your Photo

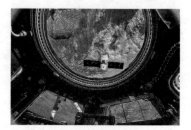

The cover photo shows the SpaceX Dragon from inside the International Space Station.

Front cover: Tim Kopra/NASA; Back cover: Science Doodle, LHF Graphics/Shutterstock.

LEARNING COMPANY

ISBN-13: 978-1-418-29162-4
ISBN-10: 1-418-29162-5
4 20

Program Authors

ZIPPORAH MILLER, Ed.D.
Coordinator for K-12 Science Programs, Anne Arundel County Public Schools
Dr. Zipporah Miller currently serves as the Senior Manager for Organizational Learning with the Anne Arundel County Public School System. Prior to that she served as the K-12 Coordinator for science in Anne Arundel County. She conducts national training to science stakeholders on the Next Generation Science Standards. Dr. Miller also served as the Associate Executive Director for Professional Development Programs and conferences at the National Science Teachers Association (NSTA) and served as a reviewer during the development of Next Generation Science Standards. Dr. Miller holds a doctoral degree from the University of Maryland College Park, a master's degree in school administration and supervision from Bowie State University and a bachelor's degree from Chadron State College.

MICHAEL J. PADILLA, Ph.D.
Professor Emeritus, Eugene P. Moore School of Education, Clemson University, Clemson, South Carolina
Michael J. Padilla taught science in middle and secondary schools, has more than 30 years of experience educating middle-school science teachers, and served as one of the writers of the 1996 U.S. National Science Education Standards. In recent years Mike has focused on teaching science to English Language Learners. His extensive experience as Principal Investigator on numerous National Science Foundation and U.S. Department of Education grants resulted in more than $35 million in funding to improve science education. He served as president of the National Science Teachers Association, the world's largest science teaching organization, in 2005–6.

MICHAEL E. WYSESSION, Ph.D
Professor of Earth and Planetary Sciences, Washington University, St. Louis, Missouri
Author of more than 100 science and science education publications, Dr. Wysession was awarded the prestigious National Science Foundation Presidential Faculty Fellowship and Packard Foundation Fellowship for his research in geophysics, primarily focused on using seismic tomography to determine the forces driving plate tectonics. Dr. Wysession is also a leader in geoscience literacy and education; he is the chair of the Earth Science Literacy Initiative, the author of several popular video lectures on geology in the *Great Courses* series, and a lead writer of the *Next Generation Science Standards**.

REVIEWERS

Program Consultants

Carol Baker
Science Curriculum

Dr. Carol K. Baker is superintendent for Lyons Elementary K-8 School District in Lyons, Illinois. Prior to this, she was Director of Curriculum for Science and Music in Oak Lawn, Illinois. Before this she taught Physics and Earth Science for 18 years. In the recent past, Dr. Baker also wrote assessment questions for ACT (EXPLORE and PLAN), was elected president of the Illinois Science Teachers Association from 2011–2013, and served as a member of the Museum of Science and Industry (Chicago) advisory board. She is a writer of the Next Generation Science Standards. Dr. Baker received her B.S. in Physics and a science teaching certification. She completed her master's of Educational Administration (K-12) and earned her doctorate in Educational Leadership.

Jim Cummins
ELL

Dr. Cummins's research focuses on literacy development in multilingual schools and the role technology plays in learning across the curriculum. *Elevate Science* incorporates research-based principles for integrating language with the teaching of academic content based on Dr. Cummins's work.

Elfrieda Hiebert
Literacy

Dr. Hiebert, a former primary-school teacher, is President and CEO of TextProject, a non-profit aimed at providing open-access resources for instruction of beginning and struggling readers, She is also a research associate at the University of California Santa Cruz. Her research addresses how fluency, vocabulary, and knowledge can be fostered through appropriate texts, and her contributions have been recognized through awards such as the Oscar Causey Award for Outstanding Contributions to Reading Research (Literacy Research Association, 2015), Research to Practice award (American Educational Research Association, 2013), and the William S. Gray Citation of Merit Award for Outstanding Contributions to Reading Research (International Reading Association, 2008).

Content Reviewers

Alex Blom, Ph.D.
Associate Professor
Department Of Physical Sciences
Alverno College
Milwaukee, Wisconsin

Joy Branlund, Ph.D.
Department of Physical Science
Southwestern Illinois College
Granite City, Illinois

Judy Calhoun
Associate Professor
Physical Sciences
Alverno College
Milwaukee, Wisconsin

Stefan Debbert
Associate Professor of Chemistry
Lawrence University
Appleton, Wisconsin

Diane Doser
Professor
Department of Geological Sciences
University of Texas at El Paso
El Paso, Texas

Rick Duhrkopf, Ph.D.
Department of Biology
Baylor University
Waco, Texas

Jennifer Liang
University of Minnesota Duluth
Duluth, Minnesota

Heather Mernitz, Ph.D.
Associate Professor of Physical Sciences
Alverno College
Milwaukee, Wisconsin

Joseph McCullough, Ph.D.
Cabrillo College
Aptos, California

Katie M. Nemeth, Ph.D.
Assistant Professor
College of Science and Engineering
University of Minnesota Duluth
Duluth, Minnesota

Maik Pertermann
Department of Geology
Western Wyoming Community College
Rock Springs, Wyoming

Scott Rochette
Department of the Earth Sciences
The College at Brockport
State University of New York
Brockport, New York

David Schuster
Washington University in St Louis
St. Louis, Missouri

Shannon Stevenson
Department of Biology
University of Minnesota Duluth
Duluth, Minnesota

Paul Stoddard, Ph.D.
Department of Geology and Environmental Geosciences
Northern Illinois University
DeKalb, Illinois

Nancy Taylor
American Public University
Charles Town, West Virginia

Teacher Reviewers

Jennifer Bennett, M.A.
Memorial Middle School
Tampa, Florida

Sonia Blackstone
Lake County Schools
Howey In the Hills, Florida

Teresa Bode
Roosevelt Elementary
Tampa, Florida

Tyler C. Britt, Ed.S.
Curriculum & Instructional
 Practice Coordinator
Raytown Quality Schools
Raytown, Missouri

A. Colleen Campos
Grandview High School
Aurora, Colorado

Ronald Davis
Riverview Elementary
Riverview, Florida

Coleen Doulk
Challenger School
Spring Hill, Florida

Mary D. Dube
Burnett Middle School
Seffner, Florida

Sandra Galpin
Adams Middle School
Tampa, Florida

Margaret Henry
Lebanon Junior High School
Lebanon, Ohio

Christina Hill
Beth Shields Middle School
Ruskin, Florida

Judy Johnis
Gorden Burnett Middle School
Seffner, Florida

Karen Y. Johnson
Beth Shields Middle School
Ruskin, Florida

Jane Kemp
Lockhart Elementary School
Tampa, Florida

Denise Kuhling
Adams Middle School
Tampa, Florida

Esther Leonard, M.Ed. and L.M.T.
Gifted and talented Implementation Specialist
San Antonio Independent School District
San Antonio, Texas

Kelly Maharaj
Challenger K–8 School of Science
 and Mathematics
Spring Hill, Florida

Kevin J. Maser, Ed.D.
H. Frank Carey Jr/Sr High School
Franklin Square, New York

Angie L. Matamoros, Ph.D.
ALM Science Consultant
Weston, Florida

Corey Mayle
Brogden Middle School
Durham, North Carolina

Keith McCarthy
George Washington Middle School
Wayne, New Jersey

Yolanda O. Peña
John F. Kennedy Junior High School
West Valley City, Utah

Kathleen M. Poe
Jacksonville Beach Elementary School
Jacksonville Beach, Florida

Wendy Rauld
Monroe Middle School
Tampa, Florida

Anne Rice
Woodland Middle School
Gurnee, Illinois

Bryna Selig
Gaithersburg Middle School
Gaithersburg, Maryland

Pat (Patricia) Shane, Ph.D.
STEM & ELA Education Consultant
Chapel Hill, North Carolina

Diana Shelton
Burnett Middle School
Seffner, Florida

Nakia Sturrup
Jennings Middle School
Seffner, Florida

Melissa Triebwasser
Walden Lake Elementary
Plant City, Florida

Michele Bubley Wiehagen
Science Coach
Miles Elementary School
Tampa, Florida

Pauline Wilcox
Instructional Science Coach
Fox Chapel Middle School
Spring Hill, Florida

Safety Reviewers

Douglas Mandt, M.S.
Science Education Consultant
Edgewood, Washington

Juliana Textley, Ph.D.
Author, NSTA books on school science safety
Adjunct Professor
Lesley University
Cambridge, Massachusetts

Earth-Sun-Moon System x

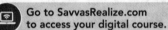

**Go to SavvasRealize.com
to access your digital course.**

▶ VIDEO
- Planetarium Technician

INTERACTIVITY
- Discovery of the Solar System
- Interpreting the Night Sky
- Patterns in Earth's Rotation
  and Revolution
- What Keeps Objects in Motion?
- Seasons on Earth
- Our View of the Moon
- Eclipses
- Moon Phases and Eclipses

VIRTUAL LAB
- Shadows in Space

ASSESSMENT

eTEXT

HANDS-ON LABS

иConnect What Is at the Center?

иInvestigate
- Watching the Skies
- Lighten Up!
- How Does the Moon Move?

иDemonstrate
Modeling Lunar Phases

TOPIC 2

Solar System and the Universe 44

The Essential Question What kind of data and evidence help us to understand the universe?

MS-ESS1-2, MS-ESS1-3

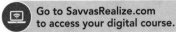

Go to SavvasRealize.com to access your digital course.

▶ **VIDEO**
- Astrophysicist

⦿ **INTERACTIVITY**
- Distance Learning
- Anatomy of the Sun
- Solar System
- How to Make a Solar System
- Space Exploration
- Telescopes
- Launch a Space Probe
- Eyes in Sky
- Star Systems
- Lives of the Stars
- Types of Galaxies
- Model a Galaxy

▤ **VIRTUAL LAB**
- A New Home

☑ **ASSESSMENT**

📖 **eTEXT**

HANDS-ON LABS

и**Connect** Planetary Measures

и**Investigate**
- Pulling Planets
- Layers of the Sun
- Space Exploration Vehicle
- How Far Is That Star?
- Model the Milky Way

и**Demonstrate**
Scaling Down the Solar System

Elevate your thinking!

Elevate Science takes science to a whole new level and lets you take ownership of your learning. Explore science in the world around you. Investigate how things work. Think critically and solve problems! *Elevate Science* helps you think like a scientist, so you're ready for a world of discoveries.

Explore Your World

Explore real-life scenarios with engaging Quests that dig into science topics around the world. You can:

- Solve real-world problems
- Apply skills and knowledge
- Communicate solutions

Quest KICKOFF

What do you think is causing Pleasant Pond to turn green?

In 2016, algal blooms turned bodies of water green and slimy in Florida, Utah, California, and 17 other states. These blooms put people and ecosystems in danger. Scientists, such as limnologists, are working to predict and prevent future algal blooms. In this problem-based Quest activity, you will investigate an algal bloom at a lake and determine its cause. In labs and digital activities, you will apply what you learn in each lesson to help you gather evidence to solve the mystery. With enough evidence, you will be able to identify what you believe is the cause of the algal bloom and present a solution in the Findings activity.

Make Connections

Elevate Science connects science to other subjects and shows you how to better understand the world through:

- Mathematics
- Reading and Writing
- Literacy

Math Toolbox

Graphing Population Changes

Ohio's Deer Population

Changes in a population over time, such as white-tailed deer in Ohio, can be displayed in a graph.

Deer Population Trends, 2000–2010

Year	Population (estimated)	Year	Population (estimated)
2000	525,000	2006	770,000
2001	560,000	2007	725,000
2002	620,000	2008	745,000
2003	670,000	2009	750,000
2004	715,000	2010	710,000
2005	720,000		

Relationships Use the data

800,000
750,000

READING CHECK Determine Central ideas
What adaptations might the giraffe have that help it survive in its environment?

Academic Vocabulary

Relate the term *decomposer* to the verb *compose*. What does it mean to compose something?

The above tablet shows:

uEngineer It! · Sustainable Design · STEM

MS-LS2-1, MS-LS2-3

Eating Oil

Do you know how tiny organisms can clean up oil spills? You engineer it! Strategies used to deal with the Deepwater Horizon oil spill, the worst in U.S. history, show us how.

The Challenge: To clean up harmful oil from marine environments

Phenomenon On April 20, 2010, part of an oil rig in

INTERACT

Design your o... clean up an oil...

Build Skills for the Future

- Master the Engineering Design Process
- Apply critical thinking and analytical skills
- Learn about STEM careers

Focus on Inquiry

Case studies put you in the shoes of a scientist to solve real-world mysteries using real data. You will be able to:

- Analyze Data
- Test a hypothesis
- Solve the Case

Case Study

MS-LS2-1

THE CASE OF THE DISAPPEARING

Cerulean Warbler

The cerulean warbler is a small, migratory songbird named for its blue color. Cerulean warblers breed in eastern North America during the spring and summer. The warblers spend the winter months in the Andes Mountains of Colombia, Venezuela, Ecuador, and Peru in northern part of South America.

Enter the Lab

Hands-on experiments and virtual labs help you test ideas and show what you know in performance-based assessments. Scaffolded labs include:

- STEM Labs
- Design Your Own
- Open-ended Labs

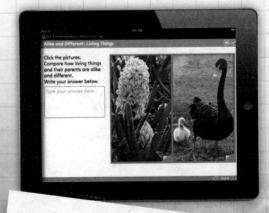

Alike and Different: Living Things

Click the pictures. Compare how living things and their parents are alike and different. Write your answer below.

Type your answer here.

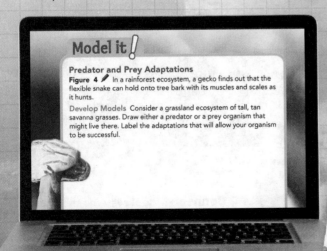

Model it

Predator and Prey Adaptations
Figure 4 In a rainforest ecosystem, a gecko finds out that the flexible snake can hold onto tree bark with its muscles and scales as it hunts.

Develop Models Consider a grassland ecosystem of tall, tan savanna grasses. Draw either a predator or a prey organism that might live there. Label the adaptations that will allow your organism to be successful.

HANDS-ON LAB

uInvestigate Observe how once-living matter is broken down into smaller components in the process of decomposition.

Earth-Sun-Moon System

NGSS PERFORMANCE EXPECTATIONS

MS-ESS1-1 Develop and use a model of the
Earth-sun-moon system to describe the cyclic
patterns of lunar phases, eclipses of the sun and
moon, and seasons.

HANDS-ON LAB

u**Connect** Model systems showing
both Earth and the sun at the center.

What is happening
to the sun?

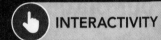 VIDEO

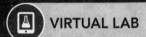 INTERACTIVITY

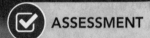 VIRTUAL LAB

 ASSESSMENT

 eTEXT

 HANDS-ON LABS

The Essential Question

How do the sun and the moon affect Earth?

CCC Patterns As the moon travels around Earth and Earth travels around the sun, the three objects interact with each other. What are some of the patterns you can observe in the interactions among Earth, the sun, and the moon?

....

....

....

....

....

....

Quest KICKOFF

How are tides related to our place in space?

Phenomenon The ebb and flow of the ocean's tides are as steady and sure as the passage of time. Engineers are investigating how to put the power of the tides to work as an alternative to the burning of fossil fuels. In this Quest activity, you will produce a model to help visitors to a tidal power company understand why tidal power is a reliable source of renewable energy. You will explore how and why our position within the solar system causes tides and their patterns. The model that you produce will demonstrate how tides happen.

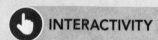

INTERACTIVITY

It's as Sure as the Tides

MS-ESS1-1 Develop and use a model of the Earth-sun-moon system to describe the cyclic patterns of lunar phases, eclipses of the sun and moon, and seasons.

NBC LEARN ▶ VIDEO

After watching the Quest Kickoff video about tidal energy, think about this source of energy. Complete the diagram by identifying some benefits and drawbacks of tidal energy.

Benefits and Drawbacks of Tidal Energy

Benefits	Drawbacks

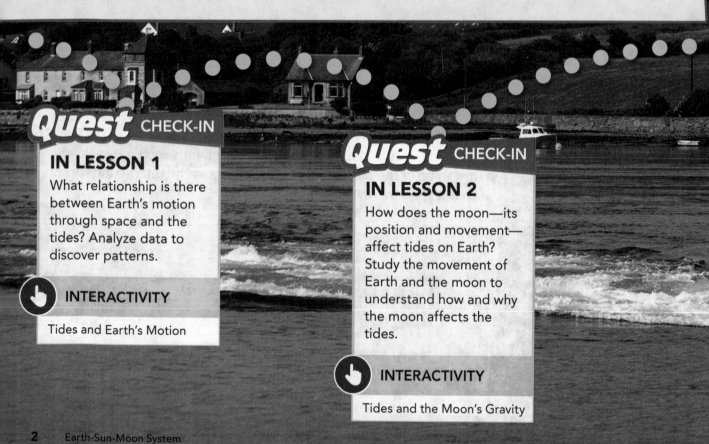

Quest CHECK-IN

IN LESSON 1

What relationship is there between Earth's motion through space and the tides? Analyze data to discover patterns.

INTERACTIVITY

Tides and Earth's Motion

Quest CHECK-IN

IN LESSON 2

How does the moon—its position and movement—affect tides on Earth? Study the movement of Earth and the moon to understand how and why the moon affects the tides.

INTERACTIVITY

Tides and the Moon's Gravity

This tidal turbine in Northern Ireland provides enough electricity to power hundreds of homes.

Quest CHECK-IN

IN LESSON 3

STEM What makes the tides and tidal ranges vary? Investigate how the relative positions of the moon, Earth, and the sun affect the tides.

HANDS-ON LAB

The Moon's Revolution and Tides

Quest FINDINGS

Complete the Quest!

Apply what you've learned to create a model that demonstrates why tides occur and how and why they provide a reliable source of energy.

INTERACTIVITY

Reflect on It's as Sure as the Tides

3

What Is at the Center?

How can you **model** Earth-centered and sun-centered systems?

Background

Phenomenon Early astronomers thought that the sun circled Earth. Astronomers have since determined that Earth circles around the sun. In this activity, you will model the two systems and evaluate whether your models give evidence to support an Earth-centered or sun-centered hypothesis.

Materials

(per group)
- flashlight
- ball

Safety

Be sure to follow all safety procedures provided by your teacher. The Safety Appendix of your textbook provides more details about the safety icons.

Design a Procedure

☐ 1. **SEP Develop Models** Use the flashlight and ball to model how the sun would move and how its light would appear to observers on Earth if Earth were at the center of the system. Describe your model in the table. **CAUTION:** *Do not shine the flashlight directly into anyone's eyes.*

☐ 2. **SEP Use Models** Move the sun and record your observations about when and where sunlight is visible to observers on Earth.

☐ 3. **SEP Develop Models** Now model how Earth would move with the sun at the center of the system. Describe your model in the table.

☐ 4. **SEP Use Models** Move Earth and record your observations about when and where sunlight is visible to observers on Earth.

Observations

Earth-centered model	Sun-centered model

HANDS-ON LAB

Connect Go online for a downloadable worksheet of this lab.

Analyze and Interpret Data

1. **SEP Construct Explanations** Based on your observations, what conclusion can you draw about the ability of observers on Earth to see the sun's light in each situation?

....

....

2. **SEP Evaluate Models** Compare your two sets of observations. From these observations, are you able to determine whether Earth or the sun is at the center of the system? What else would you need to evaluate these two viewpoints?

....

....

....

....

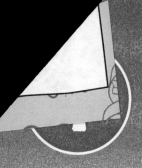

Movement in Space

Guiding Questions

- What objects can you see in the night sky?
- Why do stars in the night sky seem to move?
- How do objects in the solar system move?

Connections

Literacy Integrate With Visuals

Math Create an Equation

MS-ESS1-1

HANDS-ON LAB

uInvestigate Model how stars' positions change relative to a night sky observer on Earth.

Vocabulary

satellite
star
planet
meteor
comet
constellation
geocentric
heliocentric
ellipse

Academic Vocabulary

observations

Connect It !

✏ **Circle the meteors in this photo.**

CCC Energy and Matter Why do you think meteors leave a trail of light as they move through the sky?

....

....

The Night Sky

Why do the stars appear to move? What makes the moon shine through the darkness? Aryabhata I (ar yah BAH tah) was an early astronomer who thought about these questions. He was born in 476 CE in what is now India. Aryabhata I wrote that the moon and the planets shine because they reflect light from the sun. He came up with these conclusions based solely on his **observations** of the sky with his naked eye.

Stars, Planets, and the Moon You may look up on a clear night, such as the one shown in **Figure 1**, and see stars, the moon, planets, meteors, and comets, much as Aryabhata I did. Earth's moon is the brightest and largest object in our night sky. The moon is Earth's only natural satellite. A **satellite** is a body that orbits a planet. By contrast, stars appear as tiny points of light. However, a **star** is a giant ball of superheated gas, or plasma, composed of hydrogen and helium. As seen from Earth, the positions of stars relative to each other do not seem to change.

Have you ever noticed objects that change position from night to night against the background of the stars? These are planets. A **planet** is an object that orbits the sun, is large enough to have become rounded by its own gravity, and has cleared the area of its orbit of any debris. There are eight planets in our solar system.

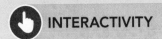

INTERACTIVITY

Answer a poll about things you have seen in the night sky.

Academic Vocabulary

How does making observations help scientists come up with new ideas?

....

....

....

....

Objects in the Sky

Figure 1 On a clear night, you can often see meteors in the night sky.

Meteors and Comets Have you ever seen a shooting star? These sudden bright streaks are called meteors. A **meteor** is a streak of light produced when a small piece of rock or ice, known as a meteoroid, burns up as it enters Earth's atmosphere. You can see a meteor on almost any clear night.

Comets are rarer sights than meteors. A **comet** is a cold mixture of dust and ice that develops a long trail of light as it approaches the sun. When a comet is far from the sun, it is frozen. As it gets close to the sun, the cloud trailing behind the comet forms a glowing tail made up of hot dust and gases.

Perhaps the most famous comet is Halley's Comet. This highly visible comet was documented by Edmund Halley, who calculated its orbit and predicted its next appearance in the sky. Sure enough, the comet appeared as he predicted in 1758, although Halley didn't live to see it. It has continued to appear about every 75 years, last appearing in 1986.

Math Toolbox

Halley's Comet

In 1910, Halley's Comet traveled close to Earth—about 1/7 of the distance from Earth to the sun. Earth's distance from the sun is 149.6 million kilometers.

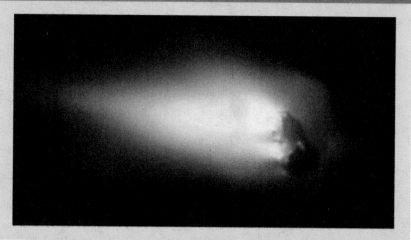

1. **SEP Use Computational Thinking** How close was Halley's Comet to Earth in 1910? Create an equation to answer the question.

....

2. **SEP Interpret Data** Estimate the next three years when Halley's Comet will appear.

....

....

3. **SEP Use Mathematics** The core of Halley's comet is oblong in shape, with its longest dimension 16 km long. Earth's diameter is about 12,700 km. How many times larger in diameter is Earth than Halley's comet?

....

....

Finding Constellations

Figure 2 ✏️ Star charts can help you to find constellations in the night sky. This is a summer chart for the Northern Hemisphere. Find these constellations in the star chart. Then write each constellation's name by its picture.

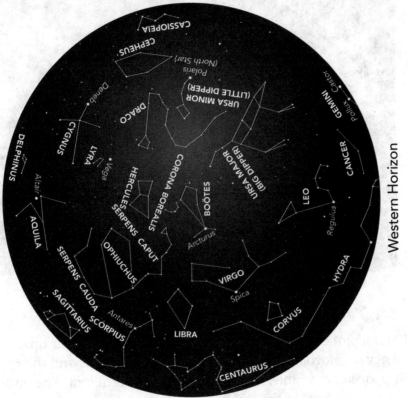

Northern Horizon

Eastern Horizon

Western Horizon

Southern Horizon

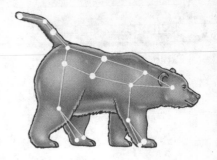

....

....

....

Constellations

For thousands of years, human beings in many cultures have seen patterns in groups of stars and given them names. A pattern or group of stars that people imagine represents a figure, animal, or object is a **constellation**. Often, as in the ancient Roman and Greek cultures, constellations supported specific mythologies. Today, scientists divide the sky into 88 constellations. Some constellations are named for people or animals from Greek myths. Pegasus and Perseus, for example, are both mythological characters and constellations. Study the constellations shown in **Figure 2**.

✓ **READING CHECK** **Integrate With Visuals** How do the pictures in **Figure 2** help you remember the constellations?

....

....

....

....

📓 **Reflect** In your science notebook, write about the patterns of stars you see in the night sky.

Star Trails

Figure 3 🖊 A time-lapse photo taken over the course of minutes or hours captures the movements of stars. The North Star happens to be aligned with the axis of Earth, directly "above" the North Pole. Circle the North Star in the photo.

Movement in the Sky

Stars, planets, and other objects appear to move over time. They do move in space, but those actual motions and their apparent, or visible, motions may be very different. The positions of objects in the sky depend on the motions of Earth.

Stars generally appear to move from east to west through the night. Toward the poles, stars appear to take a circular path, as shown in **Figure 3**. As Aryabhata I thought, this apparent motion is caused by Earth rotating toward the east. The sun's apparent motion is also caused by Earth's rotation.

Seasonal Changes Constellations and star patterns remain the same from year to year, but the constellations visible to you vary from season to season. For example, you can find the constellation Orion in the eastern sky on winter evenings. But by spring, you'll see Orion in the west, disappearing below the horizon shortly after sunset.

These seasonal changes are caused by Earth's revolution, or orbit, around the sun. Each night, the position of most stars shifts slightly to the west. After a while, you no longer see stars once visible in the west, and previously unseen stars appear in the east. After six months, Earth is on the other side of the sun. Constellations that used to appear in the night sky are now behind the sun, where the sun's bright light blocks them from our vision during the day.

Planets Planets appear to move against the background of stars. In fact, the word *planet* comes from a Greek word meaning "wanderer." Because the planets all orbit the sun in about the same plane, they appear to move through a narrow band in the sky. This band is called the zodiac.

Some planets are visible all night long. Mars, Jupiter, and Saturn are all farther from the sun than Earth is. When Earth passes between them and the sun, these three planets are visible after sunset, once the sun's bright light no longer blocks the view. You can see Venus and Mercury only in the evening or morning. They are closer to the sun than Earth, and so they always appear close to the sun, as shown in **Figure 4**.

☑ READING CHECK **Cite Textual Evidence** Why would you need two different star charts for finding constellations in the summer and the winter?

....

....

....

....

....

Mercury and Venus
Figure 4 The planets Mercury and Venus never appear far from the sun in the sky.

SEP Use Models
🖉 Where in this image is Venus farthest from the sun? Place a dot on the image to indicate the spot.

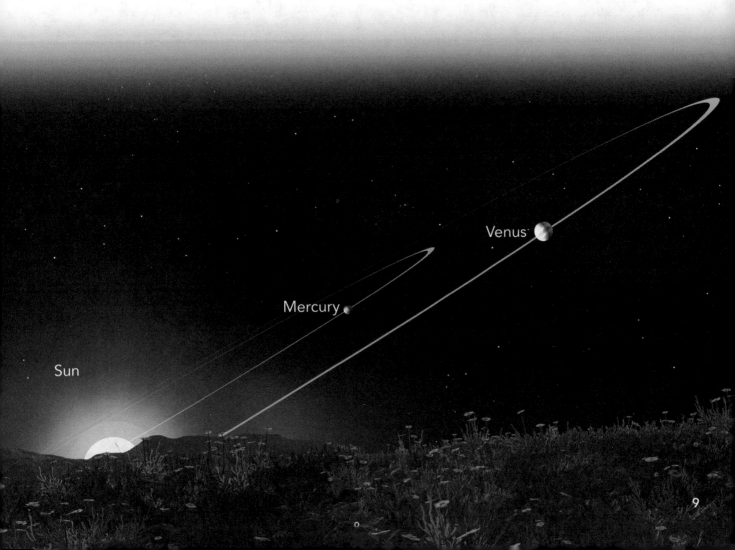

Venus

Mercury

Sun

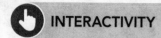
Literacy Connection

Integrate With Visuals
As you look at **Figure 5**, think about why this diagram was included on this page. Highlight the portion of the text that relates to the diagram. How does this diagram add to the information you gained by reading the text?

....

....

....

....

....

....

Models of the Solar System

From here on Earth, it seems as if our planet is stationary and that the sun, moon, and stars are moving around Earth. Ancient peoples such as the Greeks, Chinese, and Mayans noticed that although the stars seemed to move, they stayed in the same position relative to one another.

Geocentric Model Many early observers, including the Greek philosopher, Aristotle, thought Earth was the center of the universe, with all the planets and stars circling it, as shown in **Figure 5**. Because *ge* is the Greek word for "Earth," an Earth-centered model is known as a **geocentric** (jee oh SEN trik) model.

In about 140 c.e., the Greek astronomer Ptolemy further developed Aristotle's geocentric model. In Ptolemy's model, the planets made small circles called epicycles as they moved along their orbital paths. This model seemed to explain the motions observed in the sky. As a result, Ptolemy's geocentric model was widely accepted for nearly 1,500 years after his death.

The Geocentric Model
Figure 5 This geocentric model shows our solar system, with Earth in the center. The other planets orbit Earth and move along their epicycles at the same time.

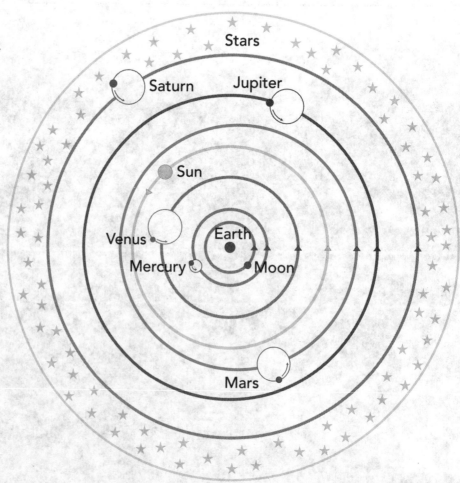

Heliocentric Model

Not everybody believed in the geocentric system. An ancient Greek scientist named Aristarchus, who lived over 400 years before Ptolemy, developed a sun-centered or **heliocentric** (hee lee oh SEN trik) model. *Helios* is Greek for "sun." In a heliocentric system, Earth and the other planets revolve around the sun. This model was not well received. Many people insisted that Earth had to be at the center of the universe.

Figure 6 lists four scientists who worked to expand and prove the heliocentric model of the solar system. The Polish astronomer Nicolaus Copernicus further developed the heliocentric model. Copernicus proposed that Earth's rotation and revolution around the sun explained the observed movements of the stars and planets. He published his work in 1543. Copernicus's theory would eventually revolutionize the science of astronomy, the study of space.

Early heliocentric models assumed that planets moved in perfect circles. Their models fit existing observations fairly well. But in the late 1500s, the Danish astronomer Tycho Brahe (TEE koh BRAH huh) made much more accurate observations. Brahe's assistant, Johannes Kepler, used the observations to figure out the shape of the planets' orbits. When he used circular orbits, his calculations did not fit the observations. After years of detailed calculations, Kepler found that the orbit of each planet is actually an **ellipse**, an oval shape, rather than a perfect circle.

Galileo's Discovery

For many years, people continued to believe the geocentric model. However, evidence collected by the Italian scientist Galileo Galilei gradually convinced others that the heliocentric model was correct. In 1610, Galileo, using a telescope that he constructed himself, discovered moons orbiting Jupiter. These Galilean moons showed that not everything in the sky travels around Earth.

Heliocentric Timeline

Figure 6 ✎ Explain what each scientist added to our understanding of the heliocentric model of the solar system.

1500

1550

1600

1650

Copernicus

....
....
....
....
....
....
....

Brahe and Kepler

....
....
....
....
....
....
....

Galileo

....
....
....
....
....
....
....

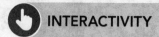
INTERACTIVITY

Determine how seasonal changes in our perception of stars support a specific model of the solar system.

Confirming the Heliocentric Model

Galileo also made other observations that supported Copernicus's theory that the sun was the center of the solar system. For example, Galileo discovered that Venus goes through phases similar to the moon's phases. But, since Venus is never too far away from the sun in the sky, it would not have a full set of phases if both it and the sun circled around Earth. Therefore, Galileo reasoned, the geocentric model did not hold true.

READING CHECK **Cite Textual Evidence** How does the development of the heliocentric model show how scientific ideas change over time?

....

....

....

....

....

Model It

Models of the Universe

SEP Develop Models Draw Galileo's heliocentric system. Show and label the evidence he produced to support his model.

1. **Predict** Two photographers take time-lapse photos of the night sky. One of them is at the equator. The other is at the South Pole. Which photo will show stars that never rise or set? Explain.

....

....

....

....

....

2. **CCC System Models** Explain the two theories about how Earth and the sun move in space relative to each other.

....

....

....

....

....

....

....

....

3. **Infer** What observations made by Galileo supported Copernicus's theory about the solar system?

....

....

....

....

....

....

....

....

4. **SEP Construct Explanations** Which patterns in space are predictable? Why?

....

....

....

5. **CCC Cause and Effect** What causes the stars to appear to move across the night sky?

....

....

....

Quest CHECK-IN

In this lesson, you learned why the stars in the night sky seem to move. You learned that various objects move, or seem to move, in space. You also discovered how Earth and the other planets move in relation to the sun.

Evaluate If the relative positions of the sun and moon affect the ocean's tides, why would it be smart for sailors and other people who work on the ocean to understand patterns in the Earth-sun-moon system?

....

....

....

👆 **INTERACTIVITY**

Tides and Earth's Motion

Go online to analyze images and data about tides and look for connections in the patterns you see.

MS-ESS1-1

THE PTOLEMAIC MODEL:
Explaining
the Unexplained

Before there were satellites and telescopes, ancient Greek and Roman astronomers relied on their eyes to learn about the solar system. Their observations led them to an understanding of the solar system in which the sun, moon, and planets revolved around Earth.

Theory from Observation

Believing he was standing at the center of the universe, astronomer Claudius Ptolemy watched planets march across the sky. But he made a few observations that intrigued him. The planets grew brighter or dimmer at times, and they seemed to speed up and slow down. Even more puzzling, some planets—such as Mars—occasionally appeared to move *backward* across the sky. If the planets circled Earth as everyone believed, how could they move so irregularly?

Ptolemy developed a theory to explain this retrograde, or backward, motion of the planets. The planets still revolved around Earth, but he argued that they moved in small circles as they traveled through a circular orbit.

Astronomer Claudius Ptolemaeus, or Ptolemy (100 CE – 170 CE), lived in Alexandria, Egypt.

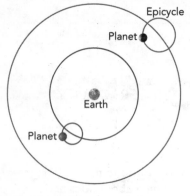

Ptolemy developed the concept of epicycles to explain why some planets appeared to move backward in their orbits. Depending on where a planet was in its epicycle, it would seem to move one way and then the other from Earth.

Advances in Technology

The Ptolemaic model was the dominant model for centuries. But astronomical instruments improved and provided more accurate measurements. Astronomers began to find errors in Ptolemy's model. In the 1500s, Copernicus proposed a heliocentric model in which the sun was the center of the solar system. Finally, Galileo used newly developed technology—a telescope—to disprove Ptolemy's model. Ptolemy hadn't been standing at the center of the universe after all.

Use the diagrams to answer the following questions.

1. **Compare** How does the geocentric model of the solar system differ from the heliocentric model?

2. **Construct Explanations** Explain how our evolving model of the solar system shows why scientists need to keep an open mind as they gather more data.

3. **Connect to Technology** Astronomers continue to refine their understanding of the solar system. How might advances in technology help to add to our knowledge?

Ptolemaic or geocentric model

Copernican or heliocentric model

Earth's Movement in Space

Guiding Questions

- How does Earth's motion affect the amount of daylight and the seasons?
- Why do Earth and the moon remain in orbit?

Connections

Literacy Cite Textual Evidence

Math Analyze Quantitative Relationships

MS-ESS1-1

HANDS-ON LAB

uInvestigate Review the differences between mass and weight and how weight is affected by gravity.

Vocabulary

axis
rotation
revolution
orbit
solstice
equinox
gravity
law of universal
  gravitation
inertia

Academic Vocabulary

hypothesize

Connect It!

✎ **Draw an X on the image to indicate the position of the sun.**

SEP Analyze and Interpret Data Which part of Earth is experiencing daytime in the image?

....

....

....

How Earth Moves

The apparent motion of the sun, moon, and stars in the sky is a result of the way Earth itself moves through space. Earth, as well as the other planets, moves around the sun in two separate ways: rotation and revolution.

Rotation To help describe Earth's movement, scientists have named an imaginary line that passes from the North Pole, through the Earth's center, to the South Pole. This line is known as Earth's **axis**, and the spinning of Earth on its axis is called **rotation**.

Look at **Figure 1**. You can see that half of Earth is lit and half is in darkness. Earth rotates from west to east (see **Figure 2**.) As it rotates, objects in the sky appear to move in the direction opposite of Earth's rotation.

As Earth rotates eastward, the sun appears to move west across the sky. As Earth continues to turn to the east, the sun appears to set in the west. Because sunlight can't reach the side of Earth facing away from the sun, it is night there. It takes Earth about 24 hours to rotate once. As you know, each of these 24-hour cycles is called a day.

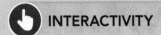

INTERACTIVITY

Investigate the patterns in Earth's rotation and revolution.

Day and Night

Figure 1 Day occurs on the part of Earth that is turned toward the sun. Night occurs on the part of Earth that is turned away from the sun.

Earth's Axis

Figure 2 🖉 Earth spins on its axis, rotating from west to east to cause day and night. Shade the part of Earth that is experiencing night.

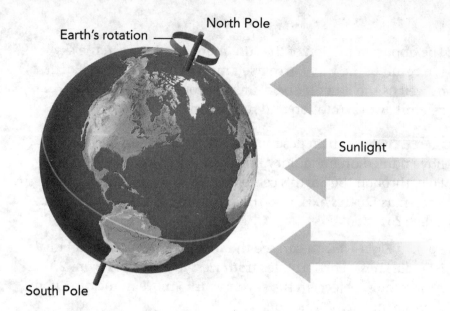

Earth's rotation

North Pole

Sunlight

South Pole

▶ **VIDEO**

Consider the difference between rotating and revolving.

Revolution As you read this page, do you feel as if you are moving? You may not feel it, but as Earth rotates, it is traveling around the sun. **Revolution** is the movement of one object around another. One revolution of Earth around the sun takes one year. Like other planets, Earth's path, or **orbit**, around the sun is an ellipse, an oval shape. The ellipse brings the planet closest to the sun in January.

Design It!

SEP Develop Models 🖉 How could you model Earth's movements? Design a model using real objects to represent Earth and the sun. Explain how you could use these objects to illustrate Earth's motions. Include both Earth's rotation and revolution in your design and explanation.

The earth is moving round the sun while it is also moving in circles, so the toy mouse is the sun going in circles while the cat chaces it round and round

The Seasons

The extent of seasonal change in any given place on Earth depends on how far away that place is from the equator. The farther away a place is from the equator, the more widely its seasonal temperatures vary. This is because of how sunlight hits Earth.

When we look at areas near the equator, we see that sunlight hits Earth's surface very directly. This sunlight is concentrated in the smallest possible area. Near the North and South Poles, sunlight hitting Earth forms a large angle with the local vertical, so the same amount of sunlight spreads over a greater area. That's why it is warmer near the equator than near the poles.

Seasonal differences in temperature are dependent on the tilt of Earth's axis. If the axis were straight up and down relative to Earth's orbit, temperatures in a given area would remain constant year-round, and there would be no seasons. However, Earth's axis is tilted at an angle of 23.5° from the vertical. Therefore, as Earth revolves around the sun, the north end of its axis is tilted away from the sun for part of the year and toward the sun for part of the year. Earth has seasons because its axis is tilted as it revolves around the sun.

Figure 3 shows how Earth moves during the year. In June, the Northern Hemisphere is tilted toward the sun and we experience summer. The sun's rays fall on a relatively small area and the temperatures are warmer. In December, the Northern Hemisphere is tilted away from the sun and we experience winter. The sun's rays fall on a relatively large area, so temperatures are lower. During March and September, sunlight strikes both hemispheres equally, causing the mild temperatures felt in spring and autumn.

Seasons

Figure 3 Earth's tilted axis affects the strength of sunlight in different places throughout the year. Which month labels the part of the diagram showing the South Pole in complete darkness?

The South pole is in complete darkness in september

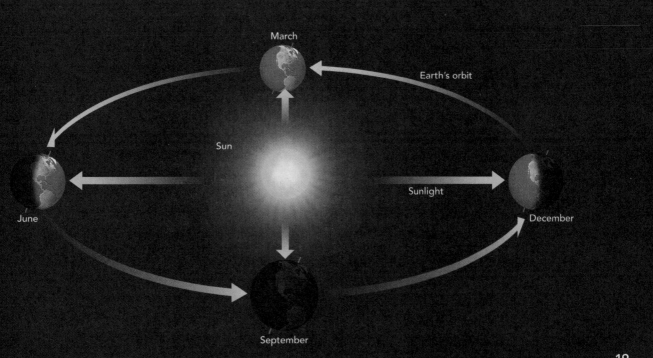

March

Earth's orbit

Sun

Sunlight

June

December

September

Day Length

The tilt of Earth's axis also affects day length. The hemisphere that is tilted toward the sun has more hours of day than night. Points on Earth near the poles have the most drastic changes in day length. In Kiruna, Sweden, shown in **Figure 4**, the sun remains below the horizon throughout the day for most of January. However, in June the sun never fully sets.

Solstices and Equinoxes

In each hemisphere, there is one day per year when the sun appears highest in the sky. Each of these days is called a **solstice**. Solstices occur when either the Northern or Southern Hemisphere is at its strongest tilt towards the sun.

Halfway between the solstices, neither hemisphere is tilted toward the sun. Each of these days is called an **equinox**, which means "equal night." This day occurs when the sun passes directly overhead at the equator at noon, and night and day are both 12 hours long.

The solstices and equinoxes occur at opposite times in the Northern and Southern Hemispheres. In the Northern Hemisphere, the summer solstice occurs around June 21, and the winter solstice occurs around December 22. However, in the Southern Hemisphere, these dates are opposite of what they are in the Northern Hemisphere. Equinoxes occur in both the Northern and Southern Hemispheres around September 22 and March 21.

Short Days

Figure 4 At noon in January, the sun is still low in the sky in Sweden.

Weightlessness
Figure 5 Astronauts experience a feeling of weightlessness when they orbit Earth because they are in freefall, with no force countering gravity. However, the inertia of their motion in orbit prevents them from falling to Earth.

Gravity and Orbits

The force that keeps Earth in orbit around the sun and the moon in orbit around Earth is the same force that prevents you from flying away when you jump. That force is gravity.

Gravity In the 1600s, an English scientist named Isaac Newton was curious about why the moon orbits Earth. In his work *Principia,* Newton contended that there must be a force, or a push and pull, acting between Earth and the moon.

Newton **hypothesized** that the same force that pulls the moon toward Earth also pulls apples to the ground when they fall from a tree. This force that attracts all objects toward each other is called **gravity**. Newton's **law of universal gravitation** states that every object in the universe attracts every other object. The strength of the force of gravity between two objects depends on two factors: the masses of the objects and the distance between them. Mass is the amount of matter in an object. Because Earth is so massive, it exerts a much greater force on you than your textbook exerts on you.

The measure of the force of gravity on an object is called weight. Mass doesn't change, but an object's weight can change depending on its location. On the moon, you would weigh about one-sixth as much as on Earth. The moon has less mass than Earth, so the pull of the moon's gravity on you would also be less. In space, as shown in **Figure 5**, you have no weight at all.

Gravity is also affected by the distance between two objects. The force of gravity decreases as distance increases. If the distance between two objects doubles, the force of gravity decreases to one-fourth of its original value.

Academic Vocabulary
How have you heard the term *hypothesize* used before?

I have when doing experements.

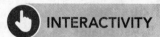
Inertia If the sun and Earth are constantly pulling on one another because of gravity, why doesn't Earth fall into the sun? The fact that such a collision has not occurred shows that a factor called inertia is at work.

Inertia is the tendency of an object to resist a change in motion. You feel the effects of inertia when you are riding in a car and it stops suddenly, but you keep moving forward. The more mass an object has, the greater its inertia. An object with greater inertia is more difficult to start or stop.

Isaac Newton stated his ideas about inertia as a scientific law. Newton's first law of motion says that an object at rest will stay at rest and an object in motion will stay in motion with a constant speed and direction, unless acted on by a force.

Math Toolbox

Gravity vs. Distance

Imagine that a spacecraft is leaving Earth's surface. How does the force of gravity between the rocket and the planet change?

Distance from Earth's Center (planet's radius = 1)	1	2	3	4
Force of Gravity on the Spacecraft (million newtons)	4	1	0.44	0.25

1. **Construct Graphs** ✏ Create a line graph of the data above.

2. **SEP Use Mathematics** What is the force of gravity on the spacecraft at twice the planet's radius from its center?

....

3. **CCC Scale, Proportion, and Quantity** What would the force of gravity on the spacecraft be at a distance of 8 radii?

....

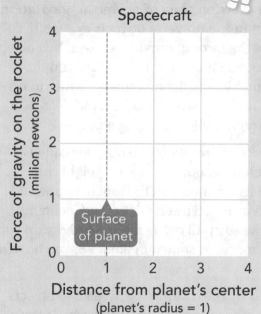

Spacecraft

Force of gravity on the rocket (million newtons)

Surface of planet

Distance from planet's center (planet's radius = 1)

Orbital Motion So, the moon travels through space at the same speed because of its inertia. But, it is constantly changing direction to remain in orbit around Earth. Newton concluded that inertia and gravity combine to keep the moon in orbit around Earth. You can see how this occurs in **Figure 6**.

Without Earth's gravity, the moon would veer away from Earth in a straight line. Earth's gravity pulls the moon inward and prevents it from moving away in a straight line. The combination of these two factors results in a curved orbital path. Similarly, planets are held in their elliptical orbits around the sun by the combined forces of gravity and inertia.

INTERACTIVI

Explore how Earth's tilte axis and revolution influence the seasons.

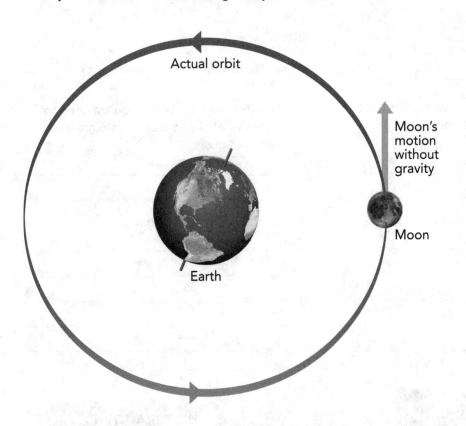

Actual orbit

Moon's motion without gravity

Moon

Earth

Orbital Motion

Figure 6 🖊 Gravity and inertia keep the moon in orbit around Earth. Complete the diagram by drawing an arrow to indicate the force of gravity Earth exerts on the moon as it orbits Earth.

✅ **READING CHECK** **Cite Textual Evidence** What factors affect the strength of the pull of gravity between two objects?

The two factors that makes the pull of gravity so much stronger is the mass of the object and the distance between the two objects.

are the two ways Earth

... earth moves from
west to east.

2. CCC Patterns What causes the pattern of day and night? What causes the pattern of the seasons?

what causes day and
night is when the earth
moves and seasons are caused
when the axsis line moves

3. Draw Conclusions What happens to the length of the day during the solstices? Why does this occur?

What happends during
the day every day when
the sun appears the
brightest. This happends
when we are directly
over the equator.

4. SEP Construct Explanations What parts of Earth generally have the highest temperatures? Which have the lowest? What causes this difference?

The top and bottom
of the earth are the
coldest and the warmest
is the middle. This is
because the middle
is clossest to the sun
and the top and bottom are

5. CCC Cause and Effect If you traveled to the the moon, what would be the effect on your farthest mass and weight?

if I went to the
moon my mass would
stay the same, but my
weight would be a
lot less.

Quest CHECK-IN

In this lesson, you learned about the way that the sun interacts with Earth to produce day, night, and the seasons. You also discovered how gravity, mass, and inertia affect the movement of Earth and the moon.

Infer When the sun, moon, and Earth are aligned, ocean tides are larger—high tide is higher, low tide is lower—than when they are not aligned. How might this relate to gravity?

INTERACTIVITY

Tides and the Moon's Gravity

Go online to study models of the motions of Earth and the moon and observe how these motions affect the tides on Earth's surface.

Tracking
Time in the Sky

Will your birthday fall on a weekend this year? Better check the calendar! A calendar organizes time into days, months, and years. It may seem like a simple grid of squares, but a calendar is actually a measurement of time based on patterns of movement among Earth, the sun, and the moon.

Egyptian Calendar (3rd Millenium BCE)

The ancient Egyptians created one of the first calendars. They figured out that a year—the time it takes for Earth to orbit the sun—was 365 days long. They used the repeating phases of the moon to divide a year into 12 months of 30 days each and tacked on five extra days at the end of the year.

Julian Calendar (46 BCE)

The Romans borrowed the Egyptian calendar, but they noticed that it didn't always line up with the first day of spring. It actually takes 365 ¼ days for Earth to orbit the sun. So, Julius Caesar added an extra day every four years to keep the calendar on track. This extra day is inserted into a "leap year," so that February has 29 days instead of 28.

Gregorian Calendar (1582 CE)

After a few centuries, it became clear that the Roman calendar also wasn't quite right. In fact, it was almost 11 minutes off each year. That may not sound like much, but by the year 1582, the first day of spring was a full ten days too early. To fix the problem, Pope Gregory XIII reset and tweaked the calendar, giving us the one we still use today.

CONNECT TO YOU

Divide this year by 4. If the year is evenly divisible by 4, it's a leap year. Years that end in 00 are exceptions. They must be divisible by 400!

The ancient Egyptians created a calendar to keep track of civic events such as festivals. Archeologists discovered this calendar in the Temple of Karnak in Luxor.

3 Phases and Eclipses

Guiding Questions

- Why does the moon appear to change shape?
- What causes solar and lunar eclipses?
- How do the sun and moon affect the tides?

Connections

Literacy Summarize Text

Math Interpret Data

MS-ESS1-1

HANDS-ON LAB

uInvestigate Research to find out why we don't see the dark side of the moon from Earth.

Vocabulary

phase
eclipse
umbra
penumbra
tide
spring tide
neap tide

Academic Vocabulary

significant

Connect It !

✏ **Observe the image of the moon in Figure 1. Draw several other shapes that you have seen the moon take.**

SEP Construct Explanations What might be causing these changes?

phases are caused by the motion of the moon around the Earth.

CCC Patterns How is Earth affected by the moon?

The earth is affected by the moon by the near side is night.

The Appearance of the Moon

When the moon is full, it shines so brightly that it makes the night sky significantly brighter. At these times, when viewed from Earth, the moon is round or almost round. Other times, the moon is just a thin crescent in the sky, seeming to emit a small strand of light, as in **Figure 1**. The different shapes of the moon you see are called **phases**. Phases are caused by the motions of the moon around Earth.

The Two Sides of the Moon
When you look at the moon when it's full, you may see what looks like a face. You are actually seeing some of the most dramatic features of the moon, a pattern of light-colored and dark-colored areas on the moon's surface. The dark-colored areas are low, flat plains of lava called *maria*. You may also be able to detect brighter patterns that indicate highland areas, often dotted with craters.

For observers from Earth these distinctive patterns on the moon never move. The side of the moon that always faces Earth is called the near side. The side of the moon that always faces away from Earth is the far side, or dark side. To find out why the same side of the moon always faces Earth, you must study the motion of the moon around Earth.

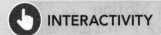

INTERACTIVITY

Investigate why the moon is sometimes visible during the day.

Reflect Look up at the sky tonight. What phase of the moon do you see? In your science notebook, track the phases of the moon. Based on your observations, what is the position of the moon in relation to the sun and Earth?

Moon Phases
Figure 1 This crescent moon appeared over the horizon shortly before sunrise.

Lunar Motion

Figure 2 🖊 This diagram shows the rotation and revolution of the moon. Add a drawing of a face on the two remaining images of the moon to show how the moon is facing Earth at each phase. <u>How would the moon appear from Earth if the moon did not rotate?</u>

if the moon didn't rotate we would see parts of the moon

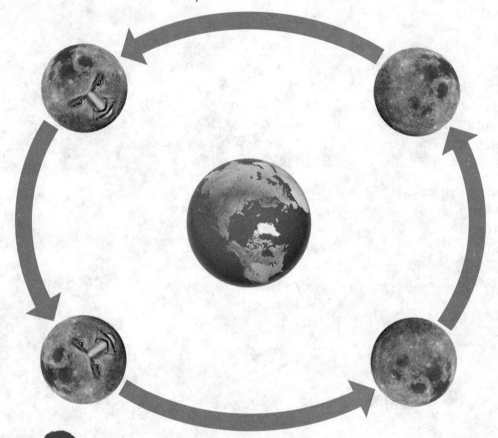

Literacy Connection

Summarize Text Underline the sentences that, if gathered together, best summarize how the sun, the moon, and Earth affect one another.

Motions of the Moon The moon, like Earth, rotates and revolves. The moon revolves around Earth and also rotates on its own axis. The moon rotates once on its axis in the same time that it takes to revolve once around Earth, as shown in **Figure 2**. Thus, a "day" on the moon is the same length as a "year" on the moon. This also explains why you always see the same side of the moon from Earth.

If you could look at the moon from space, you would see that half of the moon is always lit by the sun. The amount of the moon's surface that is lit is constant. But because the moon orbits Earth, the part of the lit surface that is visible from Earth changes. The phase of the moon you see depends on how much of the sunlit side of the moon faces Earth. These periods of light and darkness occur in predictable patterns, as shown in **Figure 3**.

Phases of the Moon

During the new moon phase, the moon is between Earth and the sun. The side of the moon facing Earth is dark and the opposite side of the moon is facing the sun. As the moon revolves around Earth, the side of the moon you see gradually becomes more illuminated by direct sunlight.

After about a week, the angle formed by the sun, moon, and Earth is about 90 degrees. This is called the first quarter moon and it is half lit and half dark. About halfway through the moon's revolution, you see the full sunlit side of the moon, called a full moon. About a week later, the sun is shining on the other half of the moon, creating a third quarter moon. At this time you see half of the lit side. After about 29.5 days, the pattern begins again and a new moon occurs.

☑ READING CHECK **Translate Information** Use **Figure 3** to describe what is happening during a waning crescent.

during a crescent moon The moon is facing the dark side of the earth and the Sun. The moon illuminates and that is why we see a creasent.

Moon Phases

Figure 3 ✎ In the empty circle, draw what a waning crescent moon looks like from Earth.

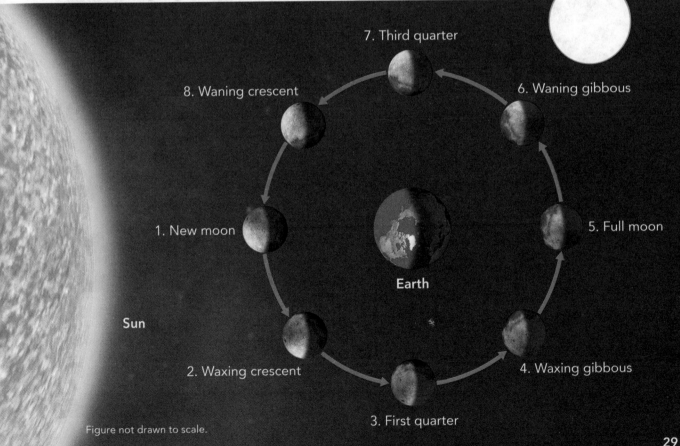

Figure not drawn to scale.

29

Two Types of Eclipses

Figure 4 ✏️ Draw an *X* on each diagram to show a spot where each eclipse can be seen. Add labels for the Earth's penumbra and umbra in the lunar eclipse diagram. Mark a *P* to show the places a moon could be during a partial lunar eclipse.

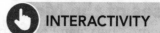
INTERACTIVITY

Use a virtual activity to learn more about eclipses.

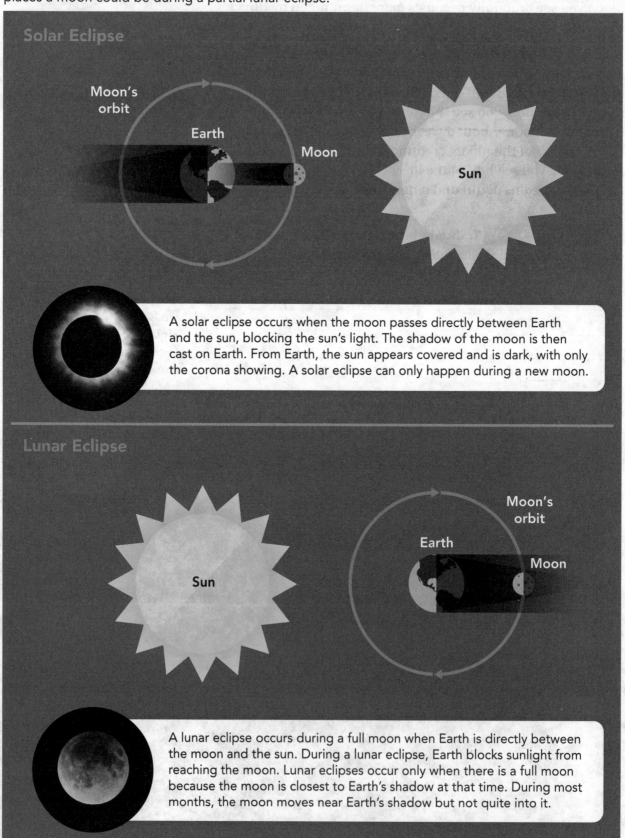

Solar Eclipse

Moon's orbit

Earth

Moon

Sun

A solar eclipse occurs when the moon passes directly between Earth and the sun, blocking the sun's light. The shadow of the moon is then cast on Earth. From Earth, the sun appears covered and is dark, with only the corona showing. A solar eclipse can only happen during a new moon.

Lunar Eclipse

Sun

Moon's orbit

Earth

Moon

A lunar eclipse occurs during a full moon when Earth is directly between the moon and the sun. During a lunar eclipse, Earth blocks sunlight from reaching the moon. Lunar eclipses occur only when there is a full moon because the moon is closest to Earth's shadow at that time. During most months, the moon moves near Earth's shadow but not quite into it.

Eclipses

When an object in space comes between the sun and a third object, it cases a shadow on the third object, causing an **eclipse**. There are two types of eclipses, solar eclipses and lunar eclipses, as shown in **Figure 4**.

Every month there is a new moon and a full moon, but eclipses don't occur every month. The plane of the moon's orbit around Earth is off by about 5 degrees from the plane of Earth's orbit around the sun. During most months, the shadow cast by Earth or the moon misses the other object.

During an eclipse, the very darkest part of the shadow where the light from the sun is completely blocked is the **umbra**. Only people within the umbra experience a total solar eclipse. The moon's umbra is fairly narrow, while Earth's is much broader. Because a lunar eclipse is visible from every point on Earth's night side, more people have a view of a total lunar eclipse than of a total solar eclipse.

The area of the shadow where the sun is only partially blocked is called the **penumbra**. During a solar eclipse, people in the penumbra see only a partial eclipse. A partial lunar eclipse occurs when the moon passes partly into the umbra of Earth's shadow. The edge of the umbra appears blurry, and you can watch it pass across the moon for two or three hours.

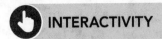

INTERACTIVITY

Learn more about the phases of the moon and eclipses.

VIDEO

Discover what it's like to work in a planetarium.

✓ **READING CHECK** **Determine Central Ideas** Why isn't there an eclipse every month?

The eclipes doesn't happen every month because the shadow from moon or sun misses it from another object.

Model It !

Solar and Lunar Eclipses

Solar and lunar eclipses occur when the sun, moon, and Earth are perfectly aligned.

SEP Develop Models 🖉 How could you represent Earth, the moon, and the sun during an eclipse? Use real objects to create a model of a solar eclipse and a lunar eclipse. Think about what you could use as a light source to represent the sun. What positions would your objects need to be in to illustrate each type of eclipse? Draw and label the plan for your models.

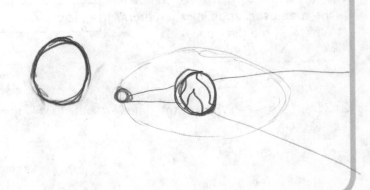

Tides

Tides are the rise and fall of ocean water that occur approximately every 12.5 hours. Tides result from gravitational differences in how Earth, the moon, and the sun interact at different alignments. The water rises for about 6 hours, then falls for about 6 hours.

The Moon and Sun The moon's gravity pulls more strongly on the side of Earth facing the moon. This pull causes the ocean water to bulge on that side of Earth. Another bulge forms on the side of Earth that is farther from the moon, where the moon's pull is weakest. This causes the formation of high tides in both locations and low tides in between. As Earth rotates, the bulges shift to remain oriented with the moon. As a result, a full rotation will result in two high-tides and two low-tides at a given location.

The sun also affects the ocean tides. Even though the sun's gravitational pull on Earth is much stronger than the moon's, the sun is so far away that the differences at the near side and far side of Earth are small. As a result, the sun's effect cannot cancel out the moon's effect, but it does influence it. Changes in the relative positions of the moon and sun affect the changing levels of the tides over the course of a month.

Math Toolbox

Tides are measured at different locations by choosing a reference height and then determining how far above that height the water rises. The table shows approximate data for high and low tides in Nag's Head, North Carolina, in November 2016.

High and Low Tides, Nag's Head, NC		
Date	High Tide (cm)	Low Tide (cm)
Nov. 21	99.9	20.3
Nov. 23	101.6	25.4
Nov. 25	109.2	17.8
Nov. 27	116.8	10.2

1. SEP Interpret Data Which tide has the greatest change in centimeters? What was the difference?

....

....

2. CCC Patterns Which of the dates was most likely the closest to a new moon? Explain.

....

....

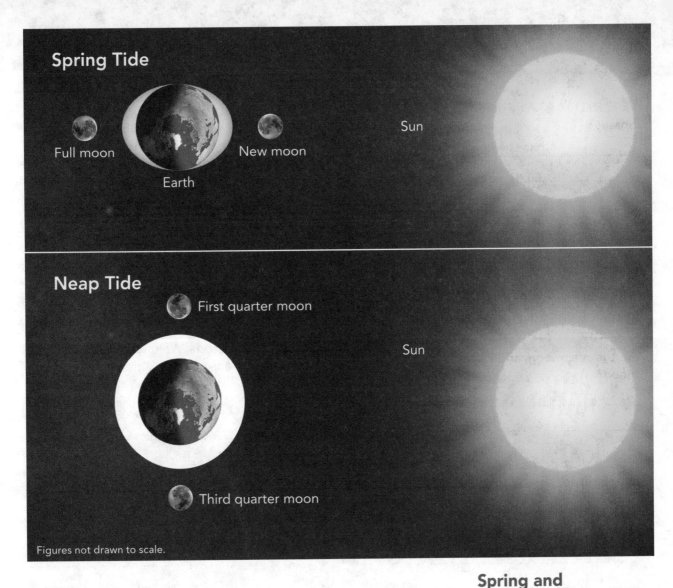

Spring Tide

Full moon

Earth

New moon

Sun

Neap Tide

First quarter moon

Sun

Third quarter moon

Figures not drawn to scale.

Spring and Neap Tides The sun, the moon, and Earth line up during the new moon and full moon phases as is shown in **Figure 5**. The gravitational pulls from both the sun and moon combine to produce a tide with the most **significant** difference between consecutive low and high tides, called a **spring tide**.

During the moon's first quarter and third quarter phases, the line between Earth and the sun is at a right angle to the line between Earth and the moon. Because the sun and the moon are pulling in different directions, their gravitational pulls partially cancel each other. This arrangement produces more moderate tides, called neap tides. A **neap tide** is a tide with the least difference between consecutive low and high tides.

☑ **READING CHECK** **Summarize Text** What causes high and low tides?

<u>high and low tides are</u>
<u>caused by the moon's gravitational</u>
<u>pull</u>

Spring and Neap Tides

Figure 5 🖊 Spring and neap tides occur twice a month. Shade in the bulges that occur during the neap tide.

Academic Vocabulary

Can you use the word *significant* in a sentence about the weather?

....

....

....

....

....

MS-ESS1-1

1. CCC Patterns Why does the moon have phases?

The moon has to do with phases because the side of the moon facing the earth is dark the the side facing the Sun is light.

2. SEP Explain Phenomena In what positions are the sun, moon, and Earth during a full moon?

The moon would be in the middle of the sun and earth.

3. CCC Cause and Effect What causes a total lunar eclipse?

When the moon and the Sun are both facing the earth

4. SEP Construct Explanations Under what circumstances might you be able to view a partial solar eclipse instead of a full solar eclipse?

You can see a part solar eclipes by watching it cross the sun for two-there hours.

5. Draw Conclusions What would you expect the tides to be like during a first quarter moon?

The quater moon tides are weaker which is called a neap tides.

Quest CHECK-IN

In this lesson, you learned about how Earth, the moon, and the sun interact to create the phases of the moon, eclipses, and tides.

SEP Evaluate Information What does the pattern among the moon's phases and the cycle of tides suggest about how reliable tidal power would be?

HANDS-ON LAB

The Moon's Revolution and Tides

Go online for a downloadable worksheet of this lab. Investigate how the position of the moon relative to Earth and the sun affects tides and to explore why some tidal ranges vary over time.

MS-ESS1-1

Power From
THE TIDES

▶ **VIDEO**

Explore the mechanics of a turbine and how it generates usable energy.

How do you generate electricity from tides? You engineer it!

The Challenge: To harness tidal power to generate electricity.

Phenomenon If you've ever had to move your beach towel further up the sand as you notice the tide coming in, you've witnessed one of Earth's greatest renewable resources. Twenty-four hours a day, the tides move millions of gallons of water along coastlines around the world.

Engineers are applying an existing technology—turbines—in a new way to generate power from moving tides. Turbines look like large fans. When placed in shallow water where the tide is strong, moving ocean water turns the turbine's blades. The spinning blades power generators to make electricity. The world's first tidal energy plant, in France, produces enough electricity to power a small city.

Tidal energy doesn't create pollution, and tides are reliable and powerful. But the technology used to harness the tides is expensive. Engineers are looking for ways to make tidal turbines more cost-effective. When that happens, harnessing tidal energy may become the wave of the future.

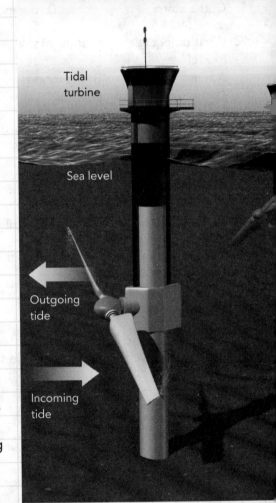

Tidal turbine

Sea level

Outgoing tide

Incoming tide

A tidal turbine generates power both when the tide comes in and when the tide goes out.

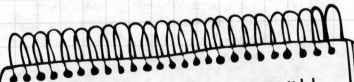

DESIGN CHALLENGE Can you design a tidal turbine? Go to the Engineering Design Notebook to find out!

1 Movement in Space

MS-ESS1-1

1. Planets appear to move in the sky against the backdrop of
A. other planets. **B.** the sun.
C. the stars. **D.** the moon.

2. What object is at the center of the geocentric model?
A. Earth **B.** the moon
C. the sun **D.** a star

3. What discovery by Galileo supported the heliocentric model?
A. the phases of Venus
B. the elliptical orbits of planets
C. the moon's orbiting of Earth
D. the movement of planets in the night sky

4. Objects in the sky appear to move due to Earth's ....

and ....

5. CCC Cause and Effect Why do stars appear to move from east to west in the night sky?

....

....

....

....

6. CCC Patterns The constellation Hercules is visible in the sky in September. Why isn't Hercules visible in the sky in March?

....

....

....

....

....

2 Earth's Movements in Space

MS-ESS1-1

7. The imaginary line that runs through Earth's pole is its
A. axis. **B.** orbit.
C. revolution. **D.** rotation.

8. Which of the following is responsible for the cyclic pattern of day and night on Earth?
A. the tilt of Earth's axis
B. the rotation of Earth on its axis
C. Earth's revolution around the sun
D. the revolution of the moon around Earth

9. Earth has seasons because
A. its axis is tilted as it revolves around the sun.
B. it rotates on its axis as it revolves.
C. the moon exerts a gravitational force on it.
D. the relative positions of Earth, the sun, and the moon do not change.

10. The two times of the year in which the sun is directly overhead at the equator are the

.... and

the ....

11. CCC Patterns How does the distance between two objects affect the force of gravity between them?

....

....

12. CCC Systems Why is it generally warmer in the Northern Hemisphere in June than it is in December?

....

....

....

....

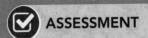

③ Phases and Eclipses

MS-ESS1-1

13. Which of the following occurs when the moon moves through Earth's shadow?
A. high tide
B. a solar eclipse
C. a lunar eclipse
D. the phases of the moon

14. When the sun, the moon, and Earth line up during a new moon, which of the following is produced?
A. low tide
B. high tide
C. spring tide
D. neap tide

15. SEP Apply Scientific Reasoning Suppose you traveled to the moon during a lunar eclipse. From your vantage point on the moon, what astronomical event would you be witnessing?

....

16. CCC Cause and Effect Why does the moon have phases?

....
....
....

17. SEP Use Models Does the diagram show a solar eclipse or a lunar eclipse? Explain.

....
....
....
....

18. Apply Concepts Which event would be less widely visible from Earth: a partial lunar eclipse or a total lunar eclipse? Explain.

....
....
....
....
....

19. CCC System Models ✏ Draw a diagram of Earth, the sun, and the moon to demonstrate the phases of the moon: new, first quarter, full, and last quarter. In your diagram, label the four different positions of the moon and sketch what the corresponding phases look like from Earth.

MS-ESS1-1

Evidence-Based Assessment

Gita is constructing a model to help her younger sister in science class. She hopes to use the model to demonstrate how the sun, Earth, and the moon interact so that her sister can describe and explain patterns in the cycles of this system. Gita wants her sister to be able to describe the following phenomena using the model:

- the phases of the moon

- the seasons on Earth

- solar and lunar eclipses

Gita's model is shown here. Gita labels E1, E2, E3, and E4 to show four positions of Earth in its orbit around the sun. She labels M1, M2, M3, and M4 to show four positions of the moon in its orbit around Earth.

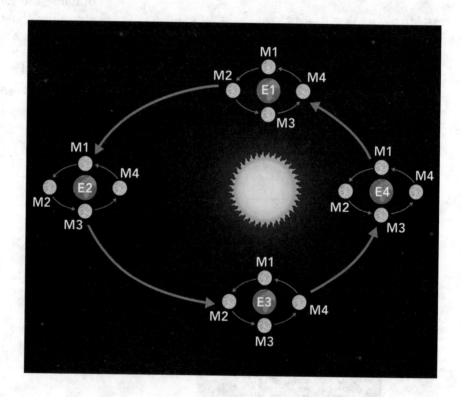

1. **CCC System Models** If Earth is at position E1 on the model and there is a new moon, then what is the moon's position?

   A. M1
   B. M2
   C. M3
   D. M4

2. **CCC Patterns** Complete the table to identify the positions of Earth and the moon in their respective orbits for each phenomenon listed.

Phenomenon	Earth's Position	Moon's Position
lunar eclipse		M4
solar eclipse	E3	
full moon	E1	

3. **SEP Use Models** Evaluate Gita's model and explain whether her sister can use it to correctly describe the patterns of the seasons on Earth.

....
....
....
....
....
....
....
....
....
....
....
....
....
....
....

4. **SEP Construct Explanations** Explain how Gita's sister can also use the model to show how patterns in the interactions among the sun, Earth, and the moon allow us to predict when lunar phases and eclipses occur.

....
....
....
....
....
....
....
....
....
....
....
....

Quest FINDINGS

Complete the Quest!

Phenomenon Think about ways to develop your model to demonstrate how the tides occur.

CCC Identify Limitations What are some of the limitations of your model for the visitor center? How could you make your model more accurate?

....
....
....

👆 **INTERACTIVITY**

Reflect on It's as Sure as the Tides

Modeling Lunar Phases

Can you **design a model** to describe how the **moon's motion** is related to its **phases**?

Materials

(per group)
- bright flashlight
- one small foam ball
- one large foam ball
- sharpened pencils or skewers

Background

Phenomenon One of the greatest achievements of our ancestors was learning to make sense of the repeating patterns in the phases of the moon. People began organizing time and planning major events, such as planting and harvesting crops, according to these cycles, resulting in the earliest stages of human civilization.

In this investigation, you will design a model, using available materials, to show the relationship between the moon's motion around Earth and the moon's phases.

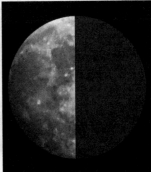

New Moon   First Quarter   Full Moon   Third Quarter

Plan Your Investigation

HANDS-ON LAB

и**Demonstrate** Go online for a downloadable worksheet of this lab.

1. You will model each view of the moon that is shown in the diagram. Look at the images of the moon. What do you think causes the differing amounts of lit moon in each image? Remember that the moon reflects light from the sun. Then think about the materials in the list. What do you think each material could represent in your model?

2. Start by discussing how you could model the view called *First Quarter*. Decide where you could position the flashlight and foam balls to show the sun, Earth, and moon in orbit. Where will you position the moon so an observer on Earth would see the first quarter moon? (Hint: Observe that during the first quarter phase, the right side of the moon is lit and the left side is dark.)

3. The next phase after first quarter is full moon. Based on this information, decide how to model the moon's orbit around Earth. In other words, in which direction does the moon orbit Earth?

4. Decide how to model the full moon, the third quarter, and the new moon. Where in its orbit does the moon take on each shape as seen from Earth?

5. Record your plans for modeling the phases of the moon. Include sketches or drawings that will help you to construct your model. Review your plans with your teacher before building and testing your model.

Plan

....
....
....
....
....
....
....
....
....
....
....
....
....

Sketches

Analyze and Interpret Data

1. **SEP Develop Models** In your model, where did you place the flashlight, large foam ball, and small foam ball to model the first quarter moon?

....

....

....

....

....

2. **CCC Patterns** Compare and contrast your models of the first quarter moon and the third quarter moon. What causes these shapes to look different to an observer on Earth?

....

....

....

....

....

3. **SEP Apply Scientific Reasoning** At the first and third quarter phases, the moon's shape appears as half a circle. Why do you think these phases are called *quarter* phases and not *half* phases?

....

....

....

....

....

4. **SEP Construct Explanations** One lunar cycle includes all of the lunar phases. One lunar cycle is about one month long. Use evidence from your model to describe how the motions of the moon lead to lunar phases that occur in a lunar cycle.

....

....

....

....

....

Solar System and the Universe

NGSS PERFORMANCE EXPECTATIONS

MS-ESS1-2 Develop and use a model to describe
the role of gravity in the motions within galaxies
and the solar system.

MS-ESS1-3 Analyze and interpret data to
determine scale properties of objects in the solar
system.

VIDEO

 INTERACTIVITY

 VIRTUAL LAB

 ASSESSMENT

 eTEXT

 HANDS-ON LABS

How do astronomers use telescopes and space probes to study the universe?

HANDS-ON LAB

и**Connect** Develop a model to compare Earth's size to the size of the other planets.

The Essential Question

What kind of data and evidence help us to understand the universe?

SEP Construct Explanations For thousands of years, people have stared at and studied the sky. Some use tools such as diagrams, telescopes, cameras, and lasers to assist them. Some have even traveled beyond Earth to take a better look. Why do you look at the sky? Why do you think others do?

....

....

....

....

Quest KICKOFF

How do we look for things that can't be seen?

STEM **Phenomenon** Telescopes and other technology allow astronomers and astrophysicists to collect data on objects in the universe. In this Quest activity, you will help with the hiring of three astronomers for a new observatory. Their specialties include asteroids, extraterrestrial life, and dark matter. In digital activities, you will investigate the work that asteroid, extraterrestrial, and dark matter hunters do. By applying what you have learned, you will develop persuasive advertisements for these positions.

 INTERACTIVITY

Searching for a Star

MS-ESS1-2 Develop and use a model to describe the role of gravity in the motions within galaxies and the solar system.

MS-ESS1-3 Analyze and interpret data to determine scale properties of objects in the solar system.

 **NBC LEARN** ▶ VIDEO

After watching the Quest Kickoff video, which examines the work of an astronomer who searches for life on planets outside our solar system, think about the qualities that make for a skilled astronomer. What scientific attitudes are important to the work of an astronomer such as the one in the video? Record your thoughts.

Qualities of a Skilled Astronomer

1 ....

2 ....

3 ....

4 ....

Quest CHECK-IN

IN LESSON 1

STEM How do astronomers study distant objects? Explore how astronomers are able to detect asteroids and the dangers these objects pose to Earth.

 INTERACTIVITY

Space Invaders

Quest CHECK-IN

IN LESSON 2

How do scientists search for extraterrestrial life in the vastness of the universe? Consider the tools they must use to look for signs of life on other planets.

 INTERACTIVITY

Anybody Out There?

IN LESSON 3

How do astronomers classify stars? Consider how studying stars helps astronomers in the search for extraterrestrial life.

Telescopes and other equipment in this observatory allow astronomers to learn more about the properties of and relationships among our close neighbors in space as well as distant galaxies.

Quest FINDINGS

Complete the Quest!

Apply what you've learned about the work astronomers do by creating a persuasive job advertisement.

 INTERACTIVITY

Reflect on Searching for a Star

Quest CHECK-IN

IN LESSON 4

STEM How do astronomers know that dark matter exists? Explore the ways in which astronomers study something that cannot be seen.

 INTERACTIVITY

Searching for the Unseen

MS-ESS1-3

Planetary Measures

Background

Phenomenon If you look at the sky at night, you might be able to spot some of the other planets in our solar system. Scientists distinguish between the inner planets, which are planets that are relatively close to the sun, and the outer planets, which are relatively far away. The planets you can see at night appear to be tiny, but that is only because they are so far away from Earth. How big are the other planets compared to Earth? In this activity, you will make a scale model to see how the other planets in our solar system compare in size to Earth.

> How can you **analyze data** to compare the sizes of Earth and the other planets?

Materials

(per group)

- quarter
- metric ruler
- butcher paper or poster board
- pencil
- compass
- pushpin
- string

Safety

Be sure to follow all safety procedures provided by your teacher. The Safety Appendix of your textbook provides more details about the safety icons.

Design a Model

1. **SEP Analyze and Interpret Data** Find information about the sizes of the planets in the solar system and record it in the table. Be sure to include the name of the dimension that you are recording and its units.

2. **SEP Develop a Model** Choose an object or quantity to represent the size of Earth in your model. Then decide how you will use the materials to represent Earth and the other planets in the model.

3. **CCC Scale, Proportion, and Quantity** Calculate the size of each of the other planets relative to the size of Earth. Then use the relative sizes that you calculated to determine the size that each planet should be in your model. Record the relative sizes and the model sizes in the data table.

4.  Build your model. To create a scale model, make each planet the model size that you have calculated it should be.

Data

Inner Planets	Mercury	Venus	Earth	Mars
Actual Size				
Relative Size Earth = 1			1.0	
Model Size				

Outer Planets	Jupiter	Saturn	Uranus	Neptune
Actual Size				
Relative Size Earth = 1				
Model Size				

Analyze and Interpret Data

HANDS-ON LAB

Connect Go online for a downloadable worksheet of this lab.

1. **SEP Analyze Data** List the planets in order from largest to smallest.

....

....

2. **SEP Analyze and Interpret Data** What difference do you see between the sizes of the inner planets relative to the sizes of the outer planets?

....

....

3. **CCC Systems and System Models** What other planetary properties could you investigate with a scale model? Explain how the model would aid in investigating these properties.

....

....

....

....

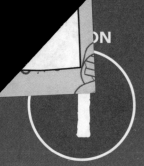

Solar System Objects

Guiding Questions

- How do the characteristics of the planets, moons, and smaller objects in the solar system compare?
- What is the role of gravity in the motions of planets, moons, and smaller objects in the solar system?
- What are the relationships between the sun and the planets in the solar system?

Connections

Literacy Integrate With Visuals

Math Convert Measurement Units

MS-ESS1-2, MS-ESS1-3

HANDS-ON LAB

uInvestigate Develop a model to describe the role of gravity in the solar system.

Vocabulary

solar system
astronomical unit
sun
planet
moon
asteroid
meteoroids
comets

Academic Vocabulary

features

Connect It !

✎ **Put an X on the object in the center of the solar system. Draw a circle around Earth.**

Use Models List all the objects you can identify.

....

....

SEP Analyze and Interpret Data What do the curved lines in the illustration represent? How can you tell?

....

....

Understanding the Solar System

Our home, Earth, is a planet. Earth is just one of many objects that make up our solar system. The **solar system** consists of the sun, the planets, their moons, and a variety of smaller objects. Each object in the solar system has a unique set of **features**. The sun is at the center of the solar system, with other objects orbiting around it. The force of the sun's gravitational pull keeps objects in their orbits around it. The strength of the gravitational force between any two objects in the solar system depends on their masses and the distance between them.

HANDS-ON LAB

Model the movements of planets around the sun.

Academic Vocabulary

The term *feature* can be used to mean a trait or characteristic. What are some features of the mode of transportation you use to get to school each day?

....

....

....

....

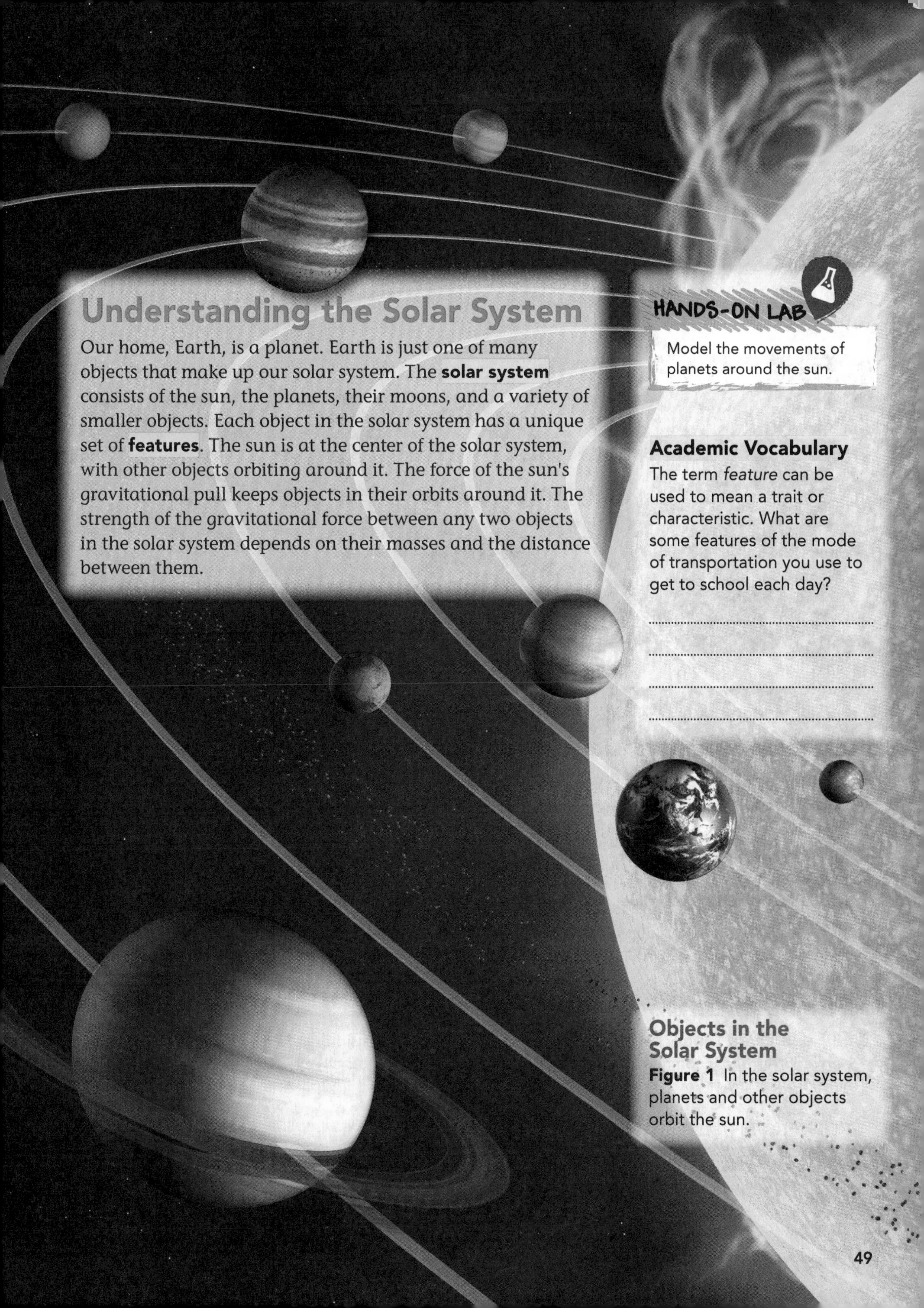

Objects in the Solar System

Figure 1 In the solar system, planets and other objects orbit the sun.

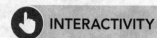
Distances in the Solar System

Distances between objects in the solar system are so large that they are not easily measured in meters or kilometers. Instead, scientists frequently use a unit called the **astronomical unit** (AU). One astronomical unit equals the average distance measured from the center of the sun to the center of Earth, which is about 150,000,000 kilometers. The entire solar system extends more than 100,000 AU from the sun.

Math Toolbox

Converting Units of Distance

✏️ Complete the diagram by drawing a line to represent the distance of 1 AU. Then write the number of kilometers equal to 1 AU.

1 AU

Earth

Sun

1 AU = [_____] km

The distances between objects in the solar system are vast. As a result, scientists use the larger value of the astronomical unit to make the numbers easier to work with.

To give you some perspective, the combined length of about 18 football fields is equal to 1 mi. One mile is about 1.6 km. That means 1 AU is equal to 1,650,000,000,000 football fields!

1. **SEP Use Mathematics** Jupiter, the largest planet in our solar system, is about 630,000,000 km from Earth. About how many AU is Jupiter from Earth?

   538.39 million

2. **SEP Use Computational Thinking** Develop your own conversion between AU and a common distance such as the length of a football field. How many of your common units is equal to 1 AU?

   18 football field = 1 AU

Comparing the Sun and Planets

Our solar system has the sun at its center. The **sun** is a gaseous body much larger than anything else in the solar system. In fact, the sun accounts for about 99.85 percent of the entire mass of the solar system. Despite being more than a million times the volume of Earth, our sun is actually a very ordinary mid-sized star. Astronomers have used telescopes to observe stars that are a thousand times more massive than the sun. Our ordinary star is expected to continue burning for another five billion years.

A **planet** is round, orbits the sun, and has cleared out the region of the solar system along its orbit. The four inner planets, including Earth, are closer to the sun, small, and made mostly of rock and metal. The four outer planets are farther from the sun, very large, and made mostly of gas and liquid. Like Earth, each planet has a "day" and a "year." A planet's day is the time it takes to rotate on its axis. A planet's year is the time it takes to orbit the sun.

☑ **READING CHECK** **Summarize Text** How do the inner and outer planets differ?

The inner planets are slower and the outer are faster

VIDEO

Learn about distances in the solar system.

HANDS-ON LAB

▢**Investigate** Develop a model to describe the role of gravity in the solar system.

Comparing the Sun and Earth

Figure 2 ✏ Circle the word that correctly completes each statement in the table.

Earth	Sun
Earth is a (star/planet).	The sun is a (star/planet).
Earth is (larger/smaller) than the sun.	The sun is (larger/smaller) than Earth.
Earth is made mostly of (gas/rock).	The sun is made mostly of (gas/rock).

Note: Sun and Earth are not to scale.

Pluto and Ida

Figure 3 Pluto (right) was considered the ninth planet in our solar system for many years. Astronomers now classify it as a dwarf planet. Asteroid Ida (top), identified in 1884, is the first observed asteroid with a moon.

INTERACTIVITY

Investigate the factors that affect the interactions of astronomical bodies.

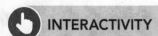

Smaller Solar System Objects A dwarf planet is an object that orbits the sun and has enough gravity to be spherical, but it has not cleared the area of its orbit. There are five known dwarf planets in our solar system: Pluto, Eris, Ceres, Makemake (MAH keh MAH keh), and Haumea (how MAY uh). As scientists observe more distant objects, they may identify more dwarf planets.

Six of the eight planets in our solar system host at least one natural satellite, or **moon**. A natural satellite is a celestial body in orbit. Just as the sun's gravitational pull keeps the planets in their orbits, the force of gravity between a host planet and its moon keeps the moon in its orbit around the planet. Mercury and Venus both lack moons. Earth comes next, with just one moon. Jupiter and Saturn each have more than 60! Some dwarf planets also have satellites.

The solar system also includes many smaller objects that orbit the sun. Some, called **asteroids**, are small, mostly rocky bodies, many of which are found in an area between the orbits of Mars and Jupiter. **Figure 3** shows an asteroid named Ida. Chunks of rock or dust smaller than asteroids are called **meteoroids**. When entering Earth's atmosphere, a meteoroid's friction with the air creates heat that produces a streak of light called a meteor. Meteoroids that pass through the atmosphere and hit Earth's surface are called meteorites. **Comets** are loose balls of ice and rock that usually have very long, narrow orbits. They develop tails as they orbit the sun.

Structure of the Sun

Recall that the sun is a gaseous body much larger than anything else in our solar system. The sun contains no solid surface, unlike our own planet. About three fourths of the sun's mass is hydrogen, and about one fourth is helium. The hydrogen and helium are in the form of plasma, a fourth state of matter. Plasma is a very hot fluid-like gas consisting of electrically-charged particles. However, like Earth, the sun has an interior and an atmosphere.

HANDS-ON LAB

Design a model of the sun's layers.

The Sun's Interior The interior of the sun includes the convection zone, the radiative zone, and the core. **Figure 4** shows the sun's interior.

Inside the Sun

Figure 4 ✏ The interior of the sun has three main layers. Draw an arrow to indicate how energy created at the sun's core travels.

The Convection Zone The convection zone is the outermost layer of the sun's interior. Plasma heated by the radiative zone rises up to the surface. The cooling plasma at the surface leads to its contraction, thereby increasing its density and causing it to sink. The heating plasma expands, decreasing its density, causing it to rise, setting up convection loops that move energy toward the surface. Cooler plasma looks darker and hotter plasma looks brighter. This creates the granular appearance of the surface of the convection zone.

Convection Zone

Radiative Zone

Core

The Radiative Zone Energy leaves the core primarily as gamma rays, which are a form of electromagnetic radiation. The gamma rays enter and pass through the radiative zone. It is called the radiative zone because most heat flows through here as forms of electromagnetic radiation. Astronomers estimate that it can take up to a million years for energy produced at the core to reach the surface of the sun. This is in part due to the incredibly high density of the plasma in the radiative zone.

The Core The sun produces an enormous amount of energy in its core, or central region, through nuclear fusion. Due to the large mass of the sun, gravitational forces place the material in the core under intense pressures, which make the core very hot. As a result, the hydrogen atoms fuse together to create helium. During this process, energy is released primarily in the form of gamma rays.

53

The Sun's Atmosphere The sun's atmosphere extends far into space, as shown in **Figure 5**. Like the sun's interior, the atmosphere is composed primarily of hydrogen and helium, and consists of three main layers—the photosphere, the chromosphere, and the corona.

The inner layer of the sun's atmosphere is called the photosphere (FOH tuh sfeer). The plasma in this layer is dense enough to be visible and directly observed. A reddish glow is sometimes visible around the edge of the photosphere. Often, this glow can be seen at the beginning and end of a total solar eclipse. This glow comes from the chromosphere, the middle layer of the sun's atmosphere. The Greek word chroma means "color," so this layer is the "color sphere." The outer layer of the atmosphere, which looks like a white halo around the sun, is called the corona. This layer extends into space for millions of kilometers.

Model It

The Sun's Atmosphere

Figure 5 This image is a combination of two photographs of the sun. One shows the sun's surface and was taken through a special filter that shows the sun's features. The other shows the corona and was taken during an eclipse.

1. **SEP Use Models** ✏ On the image, label the photosphere and the corona. Shade in and label the area of the chromosphere.

2. **SEP Develop Models** ✏ Think about how you could use commonly available materials to make a model of the sun's atmosphere. Label the layers with the materials you would use to represent them.

3. **CCC System Models** Describe two ways the materials you chose are limited in how accurately they represent the sun's atmosphere.

....

....

....

....

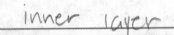

outer layer

inner layer

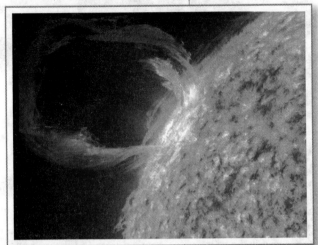

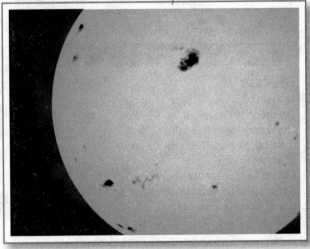

Features of the Sun

Astronomers have used special telescopes, satellites, and space probes to study the structure and features of the sun. The most visible features are sunspots, prominences, and solar flares.

Sunspots Astronomers studying the sun have observed dark areas on the sun's surface. These sunspots are areas of plasma that are cooler than the plasma around them. The cooler plasma gives off less light, resulting in the dark spots. The number of sunspots varies in a regular cycle that peaks every 11 years and corresponds to an increase in the amount of light energy given off by the sun.

Observations of the changing positions of sunspots indicate that the sun rotates, or spins on its axis. Unlike the solid Earth, which has a single rate of rotation, the sun rotates faster at its equator than near its poles.

Prominences Sunspots often occur in pairs. Huge loops of plasma that are polarized, called prominences, often link different parts of sunspot regions. Particles following these magnetic forces flow out and back on the sun's surface. You can compare sunspots and prominences in **Figure 6**.

Solar Flares Sometimes the loops in sunspot regions suddenly connect, releasing large amounts of magnetic energy. The energy heats plasma on the sun to millions of degrees Celsius, causing it to erupt into space. These eruptions are called solar flares.

✓ READING CHECK **Read and Comprehend** When prominences join, they cause (sunspots/solar flares).

An Active Star
Figure 6 Different types of photographs show the sun's different features. Label the two images above as either sunspots or prominences.

 **INTERACTIVITY**

Explore the structure of the sun.

Mercury

Mass: 0.330×10^{24} kg
Equatorial Diameter: 4,879 km
Distance from the sun: 0.39 AU
Orbital period: 88.0 Earth days
Moons: 0
Mean Temperature: 167°C
Atmospheric Composition: None (thin exosphere made up of atoms blasted off surface by solar wind)

During the day, temperatures on Mercury can reach 430°C. But without a real atmosphere, temperatures at night plunge to –170°C.

Earth

Mass: 5.97×10^{24} kg
Equatorial Diameter: 12,756 km
Distance from the sun: 1 AU
Orbital period: 365.26 Earth days
Moons: 1
Mean Temperature: 15°C
Atmospheric Composition: nitrogen, oxygen, trace amounts of other gases

Our planet is the only object in the solar system known to harbor life, mainly due to the fact that liquid water exists on its surface.

Venus

Mass: 4.87×10^{24} kg
Equatorial Diameter: 12,104 km
Distance from the sun: 0.72 AU
Orbital period: 224.7 Earth days
Moons: 0
Mean Temperature: 464°C
Atmospheric Composition: carbon dioxide (with sulfuric acid clouds)

Most planets and moons in the solar system rotate from west to east. Venus, oddly, rotates from east to west.

Mars

Mass: 0.642×10^{24} kg
Equatorial Diameter: 6,792 km
Distance from the sun: 1.52 AU
Orbital period: 687 Earth days
Moons: 2
Mean Temperature: –63°C
Atmospheric Composition: mainly carbon dioxide, with nitrogen and argon

The red planet is home to the largest volcano in the solar system, Olympus Mons.

The Solar System

Figure 7 🖊 Mark the position of each planet on the distance scale. (The planets' sizes and distances from the sun are not shown to scale.)

CCC Patterns Examine the data about each planet. What patterns do you observe?

I think that the closer the planet to the sun the more yellow it is and the farther the more blue it is

Jupiter

Mass: $1{,}898 \times 10^{24}$ kg
Equatorial Diameter: 142,984 km
Distance from the sun: 5.20 AU
Orbital period: 4,331 Earth days
Moons: 67
Mean Temperature: −110°C
Atmospheric Composition: mostly hydrogen with some helium

The Great Red Spot is one of the most noticeable features of Jupiter. This storm is so huge that two to three Earths could fit inside it.

Uranus

Mass: 86.8×10^{24} kg
Equatorial Diameter: 51,118 km
Distance from the sun: 19.20 AU
Orbital period: 30,589 Earth days
Moons: 27
Mean Temperature: −195°C
Atmospheric Composition: hydrogen, helium, and a small amount of methane

Viewed from Earth, Uranus rotates top to bottom instead of side to side. This is because the planet's axis of rotation is tilted at an angle about 90 degrees from vertical.

Saturn

Mass: 568×10^{24} kg
Equatorial Diameter: 120,536 km
Distance from the sun: 9.55 AU
Orbital period: 10,747 Earth days
Moons: 62
Mean Temperature: −140°C
Atmospheric Composition: mostly hydrogen with some helium

The particles that make up Saturn's majestic rings range in size from grains of dust to ice and rock that may measure several meters across.

Neptune

Mass: 102×10^{24} kg
Equatorial Diameter: 49,528 km
Distance from the sun: 30.05 AU
Orbital period: 59,800 Earth days
Moons: 14
Mean Temperature: −200°C
Atmospheric Composition: hydrogen, helium, and a small amount of methane

This planet just might be the windiest place in the solar system. Winds on Neptune can reach speeds of 2,000 kph.

✓ **READING CHECK** **Integrate Visuals** How does the size of the sun compare to the sizes of the planets?

....

....

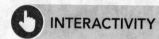
Literacy Connection

Integrate With Visuals
Use the information in the text to write a caption for the top left image in **Figure 8**.

....

....

....

Forming the Solar System

Figure 8 ✏ The solar system formed from a cloud of gas and other materials. Write the numbers 1 through 4 to put the images in order and represent how the solar system formed.

Solar System Formation

Scientists think the solar system formed at a minimum of 4.6 billion years ago from a cloud of hydrogen, helium, rock, ice, and other materials. The first step in the formation of the solar system occurred as the force of gravity began to pull together materials in the cloud. A rotating disk of gas, ice, and dust formed as the cloud material was drawn toward the central mass. As more material was pulled into the disk's center, it became more dense, pressures increased, and as a result, the center grew hot.

Eventually, temperature and pressures became so high that hydrogen atoms combined to form helium. This process, called nuclear fusion, releases large amounts of energy in the form of electromagnetic radiation, which includes sunlight.

Around the sun, bits of rock, ice, and gas began to pull together first from electrostatic charges, or electrical forces that do not flow. As the objects grew larger, gravity pulled them together. The rock and ice formed small bodies called planetesimals (plan uh TES suh muhllz). These planetesimals collided with each other and eventually created most of the objects that we see in the solar system, shown in **Figure 8**. The inner planets that formed closer to the sun were relatively smaller in size and mass. Their weak gravity, combined with the hot environment, resulted in dry, rocky bodies that were unable to hold onto light gases such as helium and hydrogen. Farther away from the sun, ice combined with rock and metal in the cooler environment. The outer planets that formed were more massive. As a result, gravity exerted a strong pull on hydrogen and helium gases, forming the gas giants we know today.

☑ LESSON 1 Check

MS-ESS1-2, MS-ESS1-3

1. **CCC Cause and Effect** What is responsible for the intense heat and pressure in the sun's core?

The reason the sun is like that is because of hydrogen and helium.

2. **CCC Systems** Describe the formation of the solar system.

The sun is in the middle. After that comes mucker, then venus, Earth, mars, Jupiter, Saturn, and uranus, and pluto. around the sun there are invisible ovals and on each oval there is a planet

3. **CCC Structure and Function** What is the relationship between a planet's distance from the sun and the length of its year? Explain.

The relaship is because the distance is what determines what year it is.

4. **Compare and Contrast** Compare and contrast asteroids, comets, and meteroids.

they are all made of rocks. Meter are the smallest. comets have ice.

5. **SEP Apply Scientific Reasoning** Explain why you think the solar system could or could not have formed without gravity.

The solar system would not be possible without gravity. because we would be falling in space without it.

Quest CHECK-IN

In this lesson, you discovered the characteristics of planets, moons, and smaller solar system objects. You also learned how the sun and other parts of the solar system were formed.

SEP Evaluate Information How do you think understanding the formation of the solar system can help to explain the presence of smaller solar system objects, such as asteroids?

....

....

....

👆 **INTERACTIVITY**

Space Invaders

Go online to explore more about the characteristics of asteroids and how scientists monitor and predict their possible strikes. Then list experience that an ideal applicant for a job at the observatory would have.

MS-ESS1-3

Comparing Solar System Objects

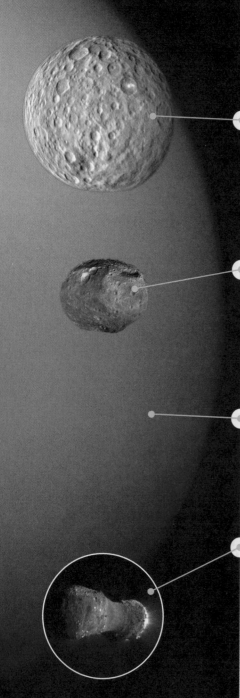

Small solar system objects far from Earth—such as comets, dwarf planets, and asteroids—have been observed for centuries. Only in recent years have astronomers been able to make observations from up close, thanks to technological advances in telescopes and spacecraft.

Ceres

A dwarf planet in the asteroid belt between Mars and Jupiter, Ceres takes 4.6 Earth years to revolve around the sun. It is about 2.8 AU from the sun. Ceres has a core of water ice and a rocky crust made of different salts. Its crust is marked by numerous impact craters.

Vesta

An asteroid in the same asteroid belt as Ceres, Vesta is made of hardened lava. About 1 percent of Vesta was blasted into space when another object collided with it, leaving a crater 500 kilometers wide. Vesta is about 530 km wide, though it is not spherical in shape.

Titan

The largest moon around Saturn, Titan has an icy surface with rivers of liquid methane and ethane. It is 9.54 AU from the sun. With a radius of 2,575 km, it is larger than Earth's moon. Its mass is 1.3455×10^{23} kg.

Hartley 2

A comet that visits the inner solar system every 6.5 years, Hartley 2, also known as 103P, is an icy mass that spins around one axis while tumbling around another. At its closest distance, Hartley 2 is about 1.05 AU from the sun, or 0.05 AU from Earth's orbit. The outer reaches of Hartley 2's orbit takes it about 5.9 AU from the sun. The comet loses some of its icy mass each time it passes near the sun.

Complete the table that summarizes the characteristics of four small objects of the solar system. Then use the information you have gathered to answer the following questions.

	Ceres	Vesta	Titan	Hartley 2
Classification	Dwarf planet	Asteroid		
Mass (kg)	9.47×10^{20}	2.67×10^{20}		3×10^{11}
Diameter (km)	952		5,150	0.16 (nucleus)
Distance from Sun (AU)		2.5		
Composition				Ice and carbon dioxide

1. **SEP Engage in Argument** Why is Vesta considered an asteroid while its "sister" Ceres is classified by astronomers as a dwarf planet?

....

....

2. **SEP Construct Explanations** Titan's average distance from the sun is 9.54 AU, which is the same as Saturn's average distance from the Sun. Why doesn't Titan crash into Saturn?

....

....

3. **SEP Develop Models** Suppose you are given a diagram that shows the position of the planets from the sun and their relative sizes. You are asked to add the four smaller solar system objects in the chart to the model. Which of the objects' characteristics would be easier to represent in the model? Which characteristics would be difficult to represent?

....

....

....

....

LESSON

(2) Learning About the Universe

Guiding Questions

- How does the electromagnetic spectrum help scientists learn about the universe?
- How do scientists use technology to learn about the universe?

Connection

Literacy Determine Central Ideas

MS-ESS1-3

HANDS-ON LAB

uInvestigate Design and build a model of a space exploration vehicle.

Vocabulary

electromagnetic
  radiation
visible light
spectrum
wavelength
telescope

Academic Vocabulary

complement

Connect It!

Study the photo and answer the questions.

SEP Analyze and Interpret Data What are some of the objects you see?

Stars and the solar system

SEP Construct Explanations How do you think astronomers took this image?

I think they took the pics
with satalights

Collecting Space Data

With advances in engineering and technology, humans discover more about the universe every year. Data from telescopes, satellites, and other instruments based both on Earth and in space are opening up the mysteries of the universe to people on Earth.

The Electromagnetic Spectrum

All objects in space emit, or give off, energy. This energy is known as **electromagnetic radiation**, or energy that can travel in the form of waves. Astronomers use instruments and tools, such as telescopes, that detect electromagnetic radiation to collect data and produce images of objects in space, such as the one in **Figure 1**.

There are many types of electromagnetic radiation, but visible light is the type that is most familiar to you. **Visible light** is the light you can see. If you've ever observed light shining through a prism, then you know that the light separates into different colors with different wavelengths, called a visible light **spectrum**. When you look at the moon or a star with the naked eye or through a telescope, you are observing visible light.

There are many forms of electromagnetic radiation that we cannot see. They include radio waves, infrared radiation, ultraviolet radiation, X-rays, and gamma rays. These waves are classified by **wavelength**, or the distance between the crest of one wave and the crest of the next wave. Radio waves have the longest wavelengths and gamma rays have the shortest wavelengths.

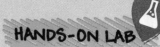

HANDS-ON LAB

Determine how lenses affect the appearance of objects seen at a distance.

 INTERACTIVITY

Explore how astronomers analyze data collected by telescopes, satellites, and probes.

Literacy Connection

Determine Central Ideas Underline the sentence that states the central idea of the text.

A Distant Galaxy

Figure 1 This image of the distant galaxy NGC 1512 is made up of several images taken by NASA's Hubble Space Telescope. This telescope is able to detect different types of objects in space.

Optical Telescopes

Objects in space give off all types of electromagnetic radiation. **Telescopes** are instruments that collect and focus light and other forms of electromagnetic radiation. Telescopes make distant objects appear larger and brighter. Some are based on Earth and others can be found floating in space. Optical telescopes use lenses and mirrors to collect and focus visible light. There are two main types of optical telescopes. Reflecting telescopes primarily use mirrors to collect light. Refracting telescopes use multiple lenses to collect light.

Other Telescopes

Scientists also use non-optical telescopes to **complement** data obtained by other methods. These telescopes collect different types of electromagnetic radiation. Radio telescopes, such as the ones in **Figure 2**, detect radio waves from objects in space. Most radio telescopes have curved, reflecting surfaces. These surfaces focus faint radio waves the way the mirror in a reflecting telescope focuses light waves. Radio telescopes need to be large to collect and focus more radio waves because radio waves have long wavelengths. Other kinds of telescopes produce images in the infrared and X-ray portions of the spectrum.

Academic Vocabulary
What does it mean when images in a book complement the text?

Radio Telescope
Figure 2 These radio telescopes are located in Owens Valley, California.

CCC Structure and function Why are radio telescopes so large?

☑ READING CHECK **Determine Central Ideas** Why do astronomers rely on different types of telescopes?

So we can see the different view points of space.

Space Probes Since humans first began exploring space, only 27 people have landed on or orbited the moon. Yet, during this period, astronomers have gathered a great deal of information about other parts of the solar system. Most of this information has been collected by space probes. A space probe is a spacecraft that carries scientific instruments to collect and transmit data, but has no human crew.

Each space probe is designed for a specific mission. Some are designed to land on a certain planet, such as the Mars rovers. Others are designed to fly by and collect data about planets and other bodies in the solar system.

Data from Probes Each space probe has a power system to produce electricity and a communication system to send and receive signals. Probes often carry scientific instruments to perform experiments. Some probes, called orbiters, are equipped to photograph and analyze the atmosphere of a planet. Other probes, called landers, are equipped to land on a planet and analyze the materials on its surface. Telescopes, satellites, astronauts, and probes have all contributed to our growing knowledge of the solar system and our universe. Space exploration is now limited only by technology, our imaginations, and the availability of funding.

HANDS-ON LAB

Investigate Design and build a model of a space exploration vehicle.

☑ READING CHECK **Determine Meaning** Why do you think spacecraft that carry instruments to collect data about objects in space are called probes?

because humans can't go to most of the planets

Plan It!

Space Probe Mission

SEP Use Models The flowchart shows the stages of a space probe mission to Mars. Write captions to describe the stages of the space probe mission.

 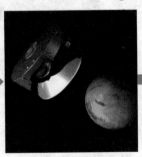  

blasting into space → _on the way to the planet_ → _entering the planet atmostphere_ → _landing on the planet_

History of Space Exploration

The advent of rocket technology in the 1940s led to a new era of space exploration, detailed in the timelines in **Figure 3** and **Figure 4**. Astronomers were no longer bound to ground-based observations, as humans, telescopes, and space probes were sent into space.

1947 Fruit Flies Launched into Space

Uncertain of the effects of space-travel on organisms, NASA begins experimentation on the effects of space exposure by launching a container of fruit flies into space to see how it affects them. Their container parachutes back to Earth and the fruit flies are recovered alive and in apparent good health.

1957 Laika Goes to Space

The Soviet Union also seeks to test the effects of space-travel on living organisms. The Soviets launch a dog named Laika into space on board a small craft called *Sputnik II*. She was the first animal ever to orbit Earth. Sadly, she died in space during the mission.

1940s

1950s

1957 *Sputnik I*

The Soviet Union launches *Sputnik I*, Earth's first artificial satellite, on October 4, 1957. This tiny craft, about the size of a beach ball and weighing little more than 80 kg, orbits Earth in 98 minutes. Its launch marks the start of the space age and a fierce space-race between the United States and the Soviet Union.

1958 *Explorer I*

The United States launches its first artificial satellite into space on January 31, 1958. Although the *Sputnik* crafts carried radio technology to signal where they were, *Explorer I* is the first satellite to carry scientific instruments into space. Its instruments help to detect and study the Van Allen Belts, strong belts of charged particles trapped by Earth's magnetic field.

1973 Skylab

Long before the International Space Station (ISS), NASA builds America's first space station, Skylab, in 1973. It orbits Earth until 1979 with the objective of helping scientists to develop science-based manned space missions. Weighing more than 77,000 kg, Skylab I includes a workshop, a solar observatory, and systems to allow astronauts to spend up to 84 days in space.

1977 Voyager 1 & 2

One of the greatest missions to explore our solar system is led by twin space-probes called *Voyager 1* and *Voyager 2*. The two spacecraft are the first human-made objects to visit the planets of the outer solar system. Their instruments help scientists to explore and study Jupiter, Saturn, Uranus, Neptune, and many of their moons.

1961 First Person to Orbit Earth

On April 12, 1961, Soviet Yuri Gagarin becomes the first person to travel into space and orbit Earth. His 108-minute mission circles the Earth once and reaches a maximum altitude of about 300 kilometers.

1960s

1970s

1962 Mariner 2 to Venus

NASA launches *Mariner 2* toward Venus on August 27, 1962. It is the first human-made object to study another planet from space. As *Mariner 2* flies by Venus, its sensors send back data on the Venusian atmosphere, magnetic field, and mass. Its instruments also take measurements of cosmic dust and solar particles before and after passing the planet.

1969 Moon Landing

Three American astronauts travel to the moon aboard *Apollo 11*. As Michael Collins pilots the command module *Columbia* above, Neil Armstrong and Buzz Aldrin land the lunar module *Eagle* on the moon and become the first humans to walk on its surface.

Space Exploration from the 1940s to the 1970s

Figure 3 🖊 Early space exploration involved some missions that carried people and some that did not. In each circle on the timeline, write *U* if the mission was unmanned, or *M* if the mission was manned.

📕 **Write About It** Scientists sent animals into space before they ever considered sending humans. In your science notebook, explain why you think humans were sent only after animals went into space.

1981 The Space Shuttles

First lifting off in 1981, the U.S. space shuttle is able to take off like a rocket and land like a plane, making it the first reusable spacecraft. Over the next 30 years, a fleet of five shuttles will be built and fly 135 missions carrying astronauts and cargo into space. Boasting a large cargo bay and lots of room for a crew, the shuttles make it possible for astronauts to launch and repair satellites, conduct research, and assist in the building of the ISS.

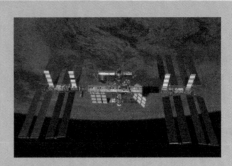

1998 The International Space Station (ISS)

Construction begins on the ISS, which requires more than 115 space flights to build. With a mass of nearly 420,000 kg, the ISS is almost five times larger than Skylab. About the size of a football field, it is the largest human-made structure ever built in space. A truly international effort, the ISS is a space-based laboratory and observatory used by scientists from around the world to conduct research that requires or focuses on the conditions found in space.

1980s

1990s

1990 Hubble Space Telescope

Carried aboard the space shuttle *Discovery* on April 24, 1990, the Hubble Space Telescope is the first space observatory located in space. Orbiting about 550 km above Earth and its blurry atmosphere, Hubble uses advanced visible-light optical technology to study the most distant objects in our solar system—stars and exoplanets in the Milky Way, as well as the farthest galaxies in the universe.

1997 Cassini-Huygens

A joint project between the United States and Europe, the Cassini mission launches on October 15, 1997, on a 3.5-billion-km journey to study Saturn, its ring system, and its many moons. Cassini also carries the Huygens Probe, which captures photos of Saturn's largest moon, Titan, while landing on its surface. The mission's many discoveries include rivers and lakes of liquid hydrocarbons on Titan's surface, making it the only known place in the solar system besides Earth where matter exists as a liquid on the surface.

2003 Mars Exploration Rovers

In 2003, NASA launches two rovers—*Spirit* and *Opportunity*—to land on and explore Mars. Their missions are to search for signs of past life. Using wheels to move around, instruments to drill and test rock and soil samples, and several sophisticated cameras, the rovers help scientists find evidence that Mars was once a wet, warm world capable of supporting life.

2009 Kepler

Seeking to answer the question of how unique our solar system is, NASA launches the Kepler Space Telescope in 2009, with instruments specially designed to search for planets outside our solar system. The Kepler mission focuses on studying a small part of the sky, counting the number and type of exoplanets it finds, and then using those data to calculate the possible number of exoplanets in our galaxy.

2000s

Present

2003 Spitzer Space Telescope

In August of 2003, NASA launches the Spitzer Space Telescope. Spitzer uses an 85-cm infrared telescope capable of seeing heat to peer into regions of space that visible-light telescopes such as the Hubble have difficulty seeing or seeing through. Using Spitzer, scientists can more easily study exoplanets, giant clouds of cool molecular gas and organic molecules, and the formation of new stars.

Space Exploration from the 1980s to Present

Figure 4 ✎ As space exploration evolved, missions changed in focus to studying more distant objects. Continue to write *U* for unmanned missions and *M* for manned missions.

CCC Patterns Describe any patterns you observe in the development of space exploration.

2012 Voyager 1 Leaves the Solar System

On August 25, 2012, *Voyager 1* leaves the area of the sun's influence and enters interstellar space, becoming the first human-made object to leave the solar system. It continues to assist scientists by transmitting data on its location and the density of plasma it encounters at the boundaries of our solar system.

....
....
....
....

☑ LESSON 2 Check

1. SEP Determine Differences Contrast the electromagnetic radiation used by radio telescopes and optical telescopes.

The difference is that the optical telescopes uses lenses in the telescope.

2. SEP Communicate Information Identify a spacecraft operated by human beings and describe how it helped add to our knowledge of space.

Some are called or- beraters which take pic. Others are called landers which analize the planet.

3. Connect to Technology Which space technology used today contributes the most to our understanding of distant stars? Explain your answer.

I think that the most space tec that is used is telescope.

4. CCC Structure and Function ✏ Choose two tools that astronomers use to learn more about objects in the universe. Draw a Venn diagram to compare and contrast how the tools function and the kinds of data they collect.

Satellite
goes into space

both
zooms in on space

Telescope
you can see space from earth

Quest CHECK-IN

In this lesson, you learned how scientists use technology to study the universe. You also discovered how the electromagnetic spectrum helps scientists to learn about objects in the universe.

SEP Engage in Argument What kinds of technology do you think would be most helpful when looking for signs of extraterrestrial life? Explain your answer.

....

....

....

⬆ INTERACTIVITY

Anybody Out There?

Go online to find out more about what extraterrestrial-life hunters look for and the technology they use. Then identify the technology with which an ideal applicant for a job at the observatory should be familiar.

MS-ESS1-3

BLAST OFF!

👆 **INTERACTIVITY**

Launch a Space Probe

How do you get a

space probe into outer space?
You engineer it! Rocket
technology shows us how.

The Challenge: To get a

space probe on its way to Pluto
and beyond.

Phenomenon In 2006, the *New Horizons* space probe was launched from Cape Canaveral, Florida. The probe was destined for the outer reaches of our solar system, studying the dwarf planet Pluto in a flyby encounter from 2015 to 2016. The Atlas V rocket was used to launch the probe on its long, 4-billion-km (2.5-billion-mile), journey. This powerful rocket, like many other rockets used to launch satellites and probes into space, is made up of two major sections called stages.

> The payload carries the *New Horizons* space probe and the second-stage Centaur engine.

> The Atlas V booster is the main part of the rocket that helps thrust the craft upward and releases it from Earth's gravitational pull.

> The solid booster rockets provide additional thrust and then fall away not long after the launch.

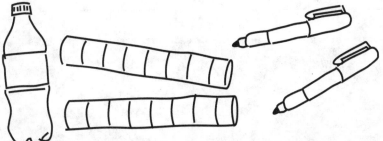

DESIGN CHALLENGE

Can you design and build a model of a rocket? Go to the Engineering Design Notebook to find out!

An Atlas V rocket on the launchpad.

(3) Stars

Guiding Questions

- What are the properties of a star?
- How do scientists classify stars?
- What is the role of gravity in the formation of a star?

Connections

Literacy Determine Central Ideas

Math Represent Relationships

MS-ESS1-2

HANDS-ON LAB

ʉInvestigate How Far is That Star?

Vocabulary

nebula
protostar
white dwarf
supernova
apparent
  brightness
absolute brightness

Academic Vocabulary

analyze

Connect It !

✏ **Write an X in the circle that points to the location of the brightest stars in the Orion Nebula.**

SEP Construct Explanations Why do you think the Orion Nebula is called a stellar nursery?

....

....

....

....

Formation and Development of Stars

Stars do not last forever. Each star forms, changes during its life span, and eventually dies. Star formation begins when gravity causes the gas and dust from a nebula to contract and become so dense and hot that nuclear fusion starts. How long a star lives depends on its mass.

All stars start out as parts of nebulas, such as the one in **Figure 1**. A **nebula** is a large cloud of gas and dust containing an immense volume of material. A star, on the other hand, is made up of a large amount of gas in a relatively small volume.

In the densest part of a nebula, gravity pulls gas and dust together. A contracting cloud of gas and dust with enough mass to form a star is called a **protostar**. *Proto-* means "first" in Greek, so a protostar is the first stage of a star's formation. Without gravity to contract the gas and dust, a protostar could not form.

Nuclear fusion is the process by which atoms combine to form heavier atoms. In the sun, for example, gravity causes hydrogen atoms to combine and form helium. During nuclear fusion, an enormous amount of energy is released. Nuclear fusion begins in a protostar.

Literacy Connection

Determine Central Ideas
As you read, look for ways that a nebula and a protostar are similar and different. Write your answers below.

....

....

....

....

....

....

The Orion Nebula

Figure 1 Stars are born in large dense clouds of gas such as this nebula located in the Orion constellation.

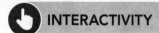
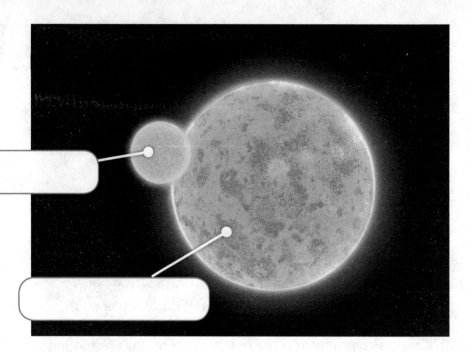

Star Mass and Life Span

Figure 2 🖊 How long a star lasts depends on its mass. Look at the yellow and blue stars. Label the star that has more mass and the star that has less mass. Predict which star will last longer by drawing an X on that star.

SEP Engage in Argument from Evidence Explain your prediction.

....

....

....

....

Life Span

The properties and life span of every star are the result of how massive it is. Each star's mass is determined by how much gas and dust condensed to form its protostar.

How long a star lasts is directly related to its mass and how quickly it uses that mass as fuel. It may seem that stars with more mass would last longer than stars with less mass. But the reverse is true. Stars are like cars. A small car has a small gas tank, but it also has a small engine that burns gas slowly. A large car has a larger gas tank, but its large engine burns gas rapidly. The small car can travel farther on a smaller tank of gas than the larger car with a large tank. Small-mass stars use up their fuel more slowly than large-mass stars, so they last much longer.

Generally, stars that have less mass than our sun use their fuel slowly and can last for up to 200 billion years. A medium-mass star like the sun will last for about 10 billion years. The sun is about 4.6 billion years old, so it is about halfway through its life span. The yellow star in **Figure 2** is similar to the sun.

Stars that have more mass than the sun, such as the blue star shown in **Figure 2**, may last only about 10 million years. That may seem like a very long time, but it is only one-tenth of one percent of the life span of our sun.

✅ **READING CHECK** **Determine Central Ideas** Describe how a star's life span is related to its size.

....

....

....

White Dwarfs

When a star begins to run out of fuel, its core shrinks and its outer portion expands. Depending on its mass, the star becomes either a red giant or a supergiant. Red giants and supergiants evolve in very different ways.

Low-mass stars and medium-mass stars take billions of years to use up their fuel. As they start to run out of fuel, their outer layers expand, and they become red giants. Eventually, the outer parts grow larger still and drift out into space, forming a glowing cloud of gas called a planetary nebula. The blue-white core that is left behind cools and becomes a **white dwarf**.

White dwarfs are about the size of Earth but about one million times more dense than the sun. White dwarfs have no fuel, but they glow faintly from leftover energy. After billions of years, a white dwarf stops glowing. Then it is a black dwarf.

Supernovas

The evolution of a high-mass star is quite different. These stars quickly procede into brilliant supergiants. When a supergiant runs out of fuel, it explodes suddenly. Within hours, the star blazes millions of times brighter. The explosion is called a **supernova**. After a supernova, some of the material from the star expands into space. This material may become part of a nebula. This nebula can then contract to form a new, partly recycled star. Nuclear fusion creates heavy elements. A supernova provides enough energy to create the heaviest elements. Astronomers think that the matter in the solar system came from a gigantic supernova. If so, this means that most of the matter around you was created in a star, and all matter on Earth except hydrogen is a form of stardust.

VIDEO

Discover how a star begins its life.

INTERACTIVITY

Examine the life cycle of a star.

White Dwarf
Figure 3 The Hubble Space Telescope captured this image of a white dwarf. The white dot in the center is the dense remaining core of the star. The glowing cloud of gas surrounds the white dwarf and eventually blows off all its outer layers.

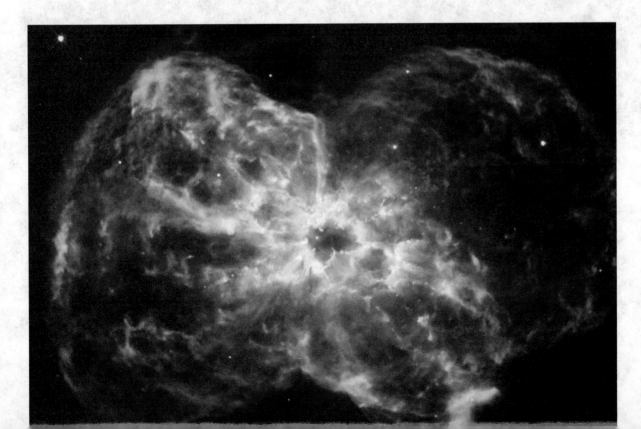

Neutron Stars, Pulsars, and Black Holes

After a supergiant explodes, some of the material from the star is left behind. This material may form a neutron star. Neutron stars are even smaller and denser than white dwarfs. A neutron star may contain as much as three times the mass of the sun but be only about 25 kilometers in diameter—the size of a city.

In 1967, Jocelyn Bell, a British astronomy student working with Antony Hewish, detected an object in space that appeared to give off regular pulses of radio waves. Soon, astronomers concluded that the source of the radio waves was a rapidly spinning neutron star. Spinning neutron stars are called pulsars, short for pulsating radio sources. Some pulsars spin hundreds of times per second!

The most massive stars—those that have more than 10 times the mass of the sun—may become black holes when they die. A black hole is an object with gravity so strong that nothing, not even light, can escape. After a very massive star dies in a supernova explosion, the gravity of the remaining mass can be so strong that it pulls the gases inward, packing it into a smaller and smaller space. The star's gas becomes squeezed so hard that the star converts into a black hole. The extreme gravity near a black hole, which is surrounded by large volumes of gas, will turn the gas into super-fast spinning disks around its equator and jets of plasma from its poles.

✓ READING CHECK

Determine Central Ideas
Will our sun become a black hole? Explain.

....

....

....

Stages of Star Development

Figure 4 🖉 Fill in the missing stages on the diagram.

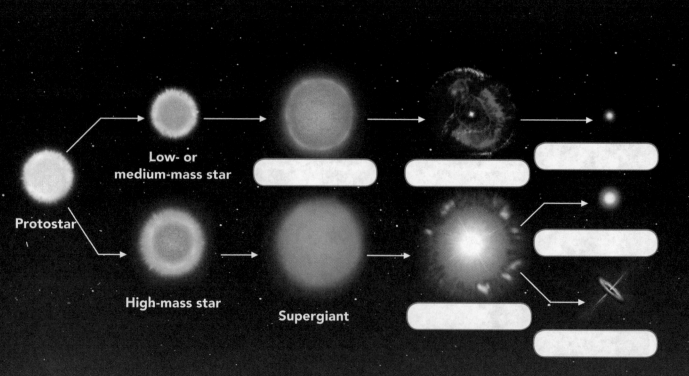

Protostar

Low- or medium-mass star

High-mass star

Supergiant

Temperature and Star Color	
Approximate surface temperature (Kelvins)	**Star color**
30,000 – 60,000 K	Blue stars
10,000 – 30,000 K	Blue-white stars
7,500 – 10,000 K	White stars
6,000 – 7,500 K	Yellow-white stars
5,000 – 6,000 K	Yellow stars
3,500 – 5,000 K	Yellow-orange stars
<3,500 K	Red stars

Source: Australia Telescope National Facility

Star Color and Temperature

Figure 5 A star's surface temperature determines its color. Look at the two stars in **Figure 2**. Use the information in the table to determine which of those two stars has the greater surface temperature. How much hotter is it than the other star?

....

....

....

....

....

Write About It Trace the evolution of a neutron star.

Star Properties

All stars are huge spheres of super-hot, glowing gas called plasma. The exact composition of this plasma varies from star to star, but it is made mostly of hydrogen. Many stars also contain varying amounts of elements such as helium, oxygen, and carbon. During its life, a star produces energy through the process of nuclear fusion, which generates energy from the process of combining atoms into larger atoms. Most stars do this by combining hydrogen atoms to form helium atoms, slowly changing their compositions over time. A star's size and composition affect its physical characteristics. Astronomers classify stars according to their physical characteristics, including color, temperature, size, composition, and brightness.

Color and Temperature
If you look at the night sky, you can see slight differences in the colors of the stars. A star's color indicates its surface temperature. The coolest stars—with a surface temperature of less than 3,500 K—appear red. Our yellow sun has an average temperature of about 5,500 K. The hottest stars, with surface temperatures ranging from 30,000 K to 60,000 K, appear bluish.

Size
Many stars in the sky are about the size of our sun. Some stars—a minority of them—are much, much larger. These very large stars are called giant stars or supergiant stars. Most stars are smaller than the sun. White dwarf stars are about the size of Earth. Neutron stars are even smaller, only about 25 kilometers in diameter.

A scientist is studying an unknown liquid in her lab. Describe a test that she could conduct to analyze a property of the liquid.

....

....

....

....

....

Chemical Composition

Stars vary in their chemical composition. The chemical composition of most stars is about 73 percent hydrogen, 25 percent helium, and 2 percent other elements by mass. Recall that nuclear fusion is the process that powers stars. This process involves the fusing of atoms to form larger atoms. In stars, this process usually involves the fusing of two hydrogen atoms to form one helium atom. As the star uses up its hydrogen, it then begins to fuse helium together, forming carbon when it reaches 100,000,000 K.

Astronomers use spectrographs to determine the elements found in stars. A spectrograph breaks light into colors and produces an image of the resulting spectrum. Today, most large telescopes have spectrographs to **analyze** light.

The gases in a star's atmosphere absorb some wavelengths of light produced within the star. When the star's light is seen through a spectrograph, each absorbed wavelength appears as a dark line on a spectrum. Each chemical element absorbs light at particular wavelengths. Just as each person has a unique set of fingerprints, each element has a unique set of spectral lines for a given temperature.

Model It

Star Spectra

Figure 6 The spectra below are from four different elements. By comparing a star's spectrum with the spectra of known elements, astronomers can identify the elements in a star. Each star's spectrum is an overlap of the spectra from the individual elements.

SEP Use Models Identify the elements with the strongest lines in Stars A and B.

SEP Develop Models ✏ Star C is made up of the elements hydrogen and sodium. Draw lines to model the spectrum of a star with this composition.

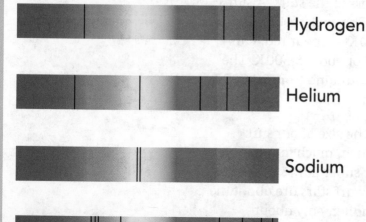

Hydrogen

Helium

Sodium

Calcium

A

....

....

B

....

....

C

Brightness Stars also differ in their brightness, or the amount of light they give off. The brightness of a star depends upon both its size and temperature. A larger star tends to be brighter than a smaller star. A hotter star tends to be brighter than a cooler star.

Astronomers use a unit called the light-year to measure the distances of stars. A light-year is the distance that light travels in one year, or about 9.46 trillion kilometers. How bright a star appears depends on both its distance from Earth and how bright the star truly is. Because of these two factors, the brightness of a star is described in two ways: apparent brightness and absolute brightness.

A star's **apparent brightness** is its brightness as seen from Earth. Astronomers can measure apparent brightness fairly easily using electronic devices. However, astronomers can't tell how much light a star gives off just from the star's apparent brightness. Just as a flashlight looks brighter the closer it is to you, a star looks brighter the closer it is to Earth. For example, the sun looks very bright. Its apparent brightness does not mean that the sun gives off more light than all other stars. The sun looks so bright simply because it is so close to Earth.

A star's **absolute brightness** is the brightness the star would have if it were at a standard distance from Earth. Finding a star's absolute brightness is more complex than finding its apparent brightness. An astronomer must first find out both the star's apparent brightness and its distance from Earth. The astronomer can then calculate the star's absolute brightness.

✓ READING CHECK **Determine Central Ideas** Our sun is a an average-sized star, yet appears brighter than others we can see. Explain why.

....

....

....

....

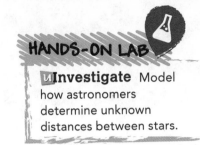

HANDS-ON LAB

и **Investigate** Model how astronomers determine unknown distances between stars.

Apparent and Absolute Brightness

Figure 7 ✏ The three stars Alnitak, Alnilam, and Mintaka in the constellation Orion all seem to have the same apparent brightness from Earth. But Alnilam is actually farther away than the other two stars. Write an asterisk (*) next to the name of the star that has the greatest absolute brightness.

Star: Alnilam
Distance: approximately 1,300 light-years from Earth

Star: Alnitak
Distance: approximately 800 light-years from Earth

Star: Mintaka
Distance: approximately 900 light-years from Earth

Classifying Stars

About 100 years ago, two scientists working independently made the same discovery. Both Ejnar Hertzsprung (EYE nahr HURT sprung) in Denmark and Henry Norris Russell in the United States made graphs to help them to determine whether the temperature and the absolute brightness of stars are related. They plotted the surface temperatures of stars on the x-axis and their absolute brightness on the y-axis. The points formed a pattern. The graph they made is called the Hertzsprung-Russell diagram, or H-R diagram.

Astronomers use H-R diagrams to classify stars and to understand how stars change over time. The diagram in the Math Toolbox shows how most of the stars in the H-R diagram form a diagonal area called the main sequence. More than 90 percent of all stars, including the sun, are main-sequence stars. Within the main sequence, the surface temperature increases as absolute brightness increases. Hot bluish stars occur at the left of an H-R diagram and cooler reddish stars are at the right.

Math Toolbox

Classify Stars by Their Properties

The H-R diagram shows the relationship between surface temperature and absolute brightness of stars.

1. **SEP Analyze and Interpret Data** 🖊 Circle the words that correctly complete the following sentence: Sirius B is a (hot/cool) star with (high/low) brightness.

2. **Represent Relationships** 🖊 Place the following stars on the H-R diagram and record their classifications below.

Star A: Red-orange, 5,000 K, high brightness

....

Star B: Yellow, 6,000 K, medium brightness

....

Star C: White, 10,000 K, low brightness

....

H-R Diagram

Star Color

| Blue or Blue-white | White | Yellow | Red-orange | Red |

High

Rigel○ ○   **Supergiants**

Betelgeuse○

Polaris○

Main Sequence

Aldebaran○

Algol○   **Giants**

Sirius A○

Alpha Centauri A○

Sun○

Alpha Centauri B

Sirius B

White Dwarfs

Absolute Brightness — Medium — Low

Surface Temperature (K): 50,000 20,000 10,000 6,000 5,000 3,000

MS-ESS1-2

1. Identify What are three properties astronomers use to describe stars?

....
....
....
....

2. Predict Which of the following will the sun eventually become: a white dwarf, neutron star, or a black hole? Explain your answer.

....
....
....
....

3. CCC Energy and Matter New stars are forming in a part of space known as NGC 346. Explain what is occurring there and the role gravity plays in the formation of these stars.

....
....
....
....
....

Use the H-R diagram in the Math Toolbox activity to help you answer Questions 4 through 6.

4. SEP Use Models The star Procyon B has a surface temperature of 7,500 K and a low absolute brightness. What type of star is it?

....
....
....

5. SEP Interpret Data Stars X and Y are both bluish main sequence stars. Star X has a higher absolute brightness than star Y. How do their temperatures compare? Explain your answer.

....
....
....
....

6. SEP Develop Models ✏ Explain why our sun is classified as a main sequence star. Then, in the space below, model the life span of our sun from its birth to its eventual final stage. Include labels that describe its color and size at each stage of your model.

....
....
....
....

 4 Galaxies

Guiding Questions

- How can we determine the sizes of and distances between stars and galaxies?
- What makes up galaxies of different sizes and shapes?

Connections

Literacy Summarize Text

Math Use Mathematical Representations

MS-ESS1-2

HANDS-ON LAB

uInvestigate Develop a model of the Milky Way.

Vocabulary

galaxy
universe
light-year
big bang

Academic Vocabulary

determine

Connect It !

✏ **Place an X on the spiral galaxies you see in this image of deep space.**

SEP Design Solutions Based on what you see, how do you think scientists measure the distances between objects in space?

....

....

CCC Scale, Proportion, and Quantity What are some challenges that you think scientists face when trying to study other galaxies?

....

....

....

From Stars to Galaxies

The brightest and largest spots of light that you see in **Figure 1** are galaxies. There are estimated to be billions of galaxies, and each of these galaxies is made up of many billions of stars. Measuring the distances between Earth and these objects poses a challenge to astronomers because the distances are so vast.

Parallax When trying to determine the distance to nearby stars and other objects, astronomers measure the object's apparent motion in the sky as Earth is on opposite sides of its orbit around the sun. This apparent motion in the object against distant background stars is called parallax.

Parallax is best used to measure the distance to nearby stars. The parallax of objects that are extremely far away is too small to be useful in obtaining an accurate measurement.

HANDS-ON LAB

Investigate Develop a model of the Milky Way.

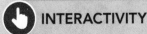

INTERACTIVITY

Find out how Hollywood goes to space.

Deep in Space

Figure 1 The universe is enormous, almost beyond imagination. This image was captured by the Hubble Space Telescope in 1995 while peering into one of the darkest regions of space as seen from Earth. Astronomers were amazed to see more than 3,000 galaxies in the tiny patch of sky captured by the orbiting observatory.

Star Systems

Many stars are part of groups of two or more stars, called star systems. Star systems that have two stars are called double stars or binary stars. Groups of three or more stars are called multiple star systems.

Often one star in a binary system is much brighter and more massive than the other. Even if only one star can be seen from Earth, astronomers can often detect its dimmer partner by observing the effects of its gravity. As a dim companion star revolves around a bright star, its gravity causes the bright star to wobble. In 1995, astronomers first discovered an exoplanet—one outside our own solar system—revolving around a star. Again, they detected the planet by observing the effect the planet's gravity had on the star it orbited.

Model It!

Eclipsing Binary Stars

Figure 2 A dim star may pass in front of a brighter star and block it. A system in which one dim star eclipses the light from another periodically is called an eclipsing binary. Scientists can measure the brightness of the brighter star and determine when the dim star is eclipsing it.

SEP Develop Models ✏ Use the information in the graph to complete the missing panels in the diagram. Indicate the positions of each of the stars in the binary system.

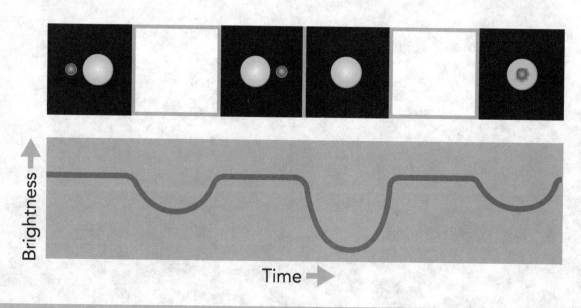

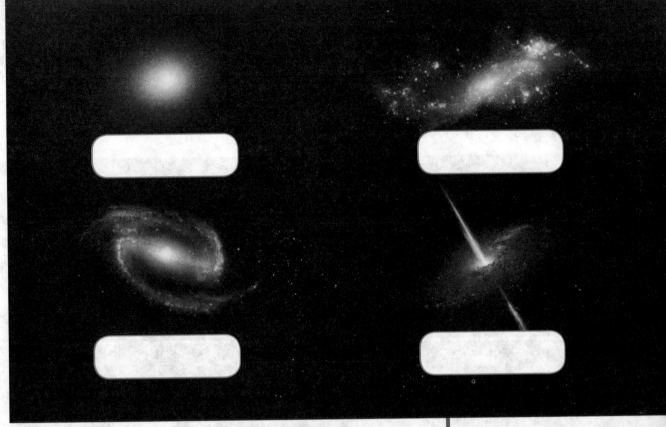

Star Clusters

Many stars belong to larger groupings called clusters. All of the stars in a particular cluster formed from the same nebula at about the same time. An open cluster looks loose and disorganized. These clusters may contain up to a few thousand stars. They also contain a lot of gas and dust. Globular clusters are large groupings of older stars. They are round and may have more than a million stars.

Galaxies

A **galaxy** is a group of single stars, star systems, star clusters, dust, and gas bound together by gravity. **Figure 3** shows several common types of galaxies. Spiral galaxies appear to have a bulge in the middle and arms that spiral outward like pinwheels. Our solar system is located in a spiral galaxy that we have named the Milky Way. Elliptical galaxies are rounded but may be elongated and slightly flattened. They contain billions of stars but have little gas or dust between the stars. Stars are no longer forming inside them, so they contain only old stars. Irregular galaxies do not have regular shapes. They are smaller than spiral or elliptical galaxies. They contain young, bright stars and include a lot of gas and dust to form new ones. Quasars are active, young galaxies with black holes at their center. Gas spins around the black hole, heats up, and glows.

☑ READING CHECK **Summarize Text** How are stars, star systems, star clusters, and galaxies related?

....

....

Kinds of Galaxies
Figure 3 ✏ From what you know about the shapes of galaxies, label each galaxy.

👆 **INTERACTIVITY**

Explore the different types of galaxies.

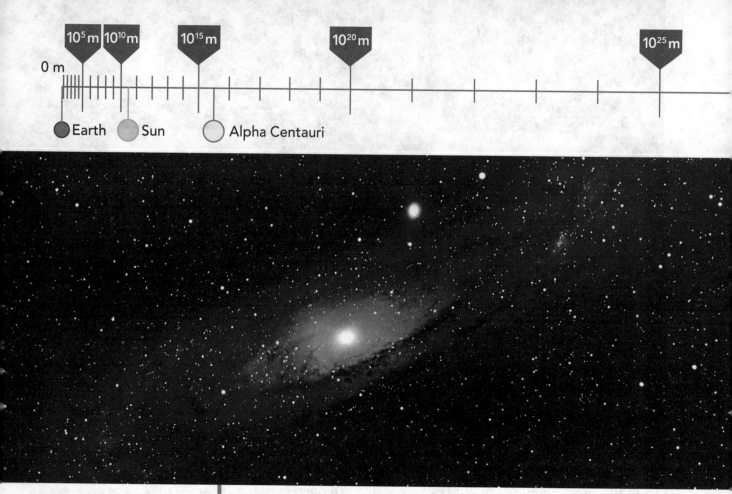

The distance scale shows markers at 10^5 m, 10^{10} m, 10^{15} m, 10^{20} m, and 10^{25} m, starting from 0 m. Earth, Sun, and Alpha Centauri are labeled along the scale.

The Andromeda Galaxy

Figure 4 ✏ Our nearest galactic neighbor is a giant spiral galaxy similar to the Milky Way called the Andromeda Galaxy. It is 2.5×10^{22} meters away. Draw where the Andromeda Galaxy should appear on the distance scale shown.

The Universe

Astronomers define the **universe** as all of space and everything in it. They study objects as close as the moon and as far away as quasars, the farthest known objects in the universe. Their research also looks at incredibly large objects, such as clusters of galaxies that are millions of light-years across. They also study tiny particles, such as the atoms within stars.

Light-Years Distances to the stars are so large that meters are not very practical units. In space, light travels at a speed of about 300,000,000 meters per second. A **light-year** is the distance that light travels in one year, about 9.46 trillion kilometers. The light-year is a unit of distance, not time. Imagine it this way. If you bicycle at a speed of 10 kilometers per hour, it would take you 1 hour to go to a mall 10 kilometers away. You could say that the mall is "1 bicycle-hour" away.

Scientific Notation As shown in **Figure 4**, the numbers that astronomers use are often very large or very small, so they frequently use scientific notation to describe sizes and distances in the universe. Scientific notation uses powers of ten to write very large or very small numbers in shorter form. Each number is written as the product of a number between 1 and 10 and a power of 10.

The Scale of the Universe
Human beings have wondered about the size and distance of the night sky throughout history. Aristarchus of Samos began questioning how far the moon was from Earth as early as the third century BCE. He used the shadow of Earth on the moon during a lunar eclipse to come up with a figure for the distance that was surprisingly accurate.

Edmond Halley is a well-known early astronomer who honed his skills in the 1600s and 1700s. He found a way to measure the distance to the sun and to the planet Venus. He did this by closely observing and measuring the shift of Venus in the sky. His discoveries helped later scientists to **determine** a more accurate scale of the entire solar system.

Academic Vocabulary
What difficulties did scientists have when they tried to determine the size of the universe? Explain some ways you can determine the size of something.

....

....

....

....

....

....

☑ READING CHECK **Determine Central Ideas** What is the reason astronomers choose to write the measurements of the universe in scientific notation?

....

....

Math Toolbox

Scientific Notation

One light-year is about 9,460,000,000,000 km. To express this number in scientific notation, first insert a decimal point in the original number to write a number between one and ten. To determine the power of ten, count the number of places that the decimal point moved. Because there are 12 digits after the first digit, the distance be written as 9.46×10^{12} km.

CCC Scale, Proportion, and Quantity Convert the following numbers from light-years to km. Then express the numbers using scientific notation.

The Andromeda Galaxy is the closest major galaxy to the Milky Way. It is about 2,500,000 light-years from our galaxy, and its diameter is estimated to be 220,000 light-years.

2,500,000 light-years = ...

220,000 light-years = ...

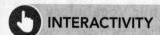

INTERACTIVITY

Design a hierarchical model of a galaxy.

VIDEO

Find out more about the big bang theory.

Understanding the Universe

Astronomers theorize that the universe began between 13.77 and 13.82 billion years ago. At that time, the part of the universe we can see was no larger than the period at the end of this sentence.

The Big Bang The universe then exploded in what has been called the **big bang**. The big bang theory states that the universe formed in an instant, billions of years ago, in an enormous explosion. New observations lead many astronomers to conclude that the universe is expanding and will likely expand forever.

The Future of the Universe In the 1920s, American astronomer Edwin Hubble discovered that almost all galaxies are moving away from Earth and from each other. Hubble's law states that the farther away a galaxy is, the faster it is moving away from us.

Other researchers believe that the force of gravity will begin to pull the galaxies back together into a reverse big bang. The universe would be crushed in an enormous black hole, called the big crunch.

Until recently, astronomers assumed that the universe consisted solely of the matter they could observe directly. But astronomer Vera Rubin discovered that the matter astronomers can see may make up as little as ten percent of the mass in the galaxies. The rest exists in the form of dark matter. Dark matter is matter that does not give off electromagnetic radiation. It cannot be seen directly. However, its presence can be inferred by observing the effect of its gravity on visible objects within a rotating galaxy.

In the late 1990s, astronomers observed that the expansion of the universe appeared to be accelerating. Astronomers infer that a mysterious new force, which they call dark energy, may be causing the expansion of the universe to increase.

READING CHECK **Determine Central Ideas** How does Hubble's law support the big bang theory?

....

....

....

....

Literacy Connection

Summarize Text What is dark matter?

....

....

....

....

How the Universe Formed

Figure 5 This diagram illustrates how astronomers theorize that the universe began and will continue. How does the idea of an expanding universe support the big bang theory?

....
....
....
....
....
....
....

Big Bang

Today

Time ⟶

☑LESSON 4 Check

MS-ESS1-2

1. **Identify** What are the four types of galaxies?

....

....

....

....

2. **CCC Cause and Effect** How can astronomers detect a binary star if only one of the two stars is visible from Earth?

....

....

....

....

....

3. **SEP Interpret Data** The speed of light is 3.0×10^8 m/s when expressed in scientific notation. How would you express this in real numbers?

....

....

....

4. **SEP Evaluate Information** A friend uses an analogy of raisins in rising bread dough to describe galaxies in the expanding universe. Is your friend correct? Explain.

....

....

....

....

....

....

....

5. **Estimate** Based on what astronomers currently know, how old is our universe?

....

....

....

....

....

....

Quest CHECK-IN

In this lesson, you learned about how astronomers determine the distances between objects. You also learned about how they think the universe began and how it will continue in the future.

Draw Conclusions Why is it important for astronomers to be able to make inferences when interpreting data about things they cannot observe directly?

....

....

....

....

....

INTERACTIVITY

Searching for the Unseen

Go online to explore how scientists know dark matter exists even though they cannot see it. Then begin developing the job descriptions for the new positions at the observatory.

MS-ESS1-2

Traveling Through the
Milky Way

The Milky Way is a spiral galaxy 100,000 light-years wide. Our solar system is a small speck on one of the arms that spirals out from the center of the galaxy. Just as the planets of our solar system revolve around the sun due to gravity, the entire solar system orbits the center of the Milky Way due to the force of gravity.

Our solar system moves at 240 kilometers per second around the center of the Milky Way. At this speed, it takes 250 million Earth years for our solar system to travel all the way around!

Modern astronomy uses sophisticated tools to measure distances among objects in the Milky Way, and also to identify those objects. The Kepler space telescope, launched into Earth's orbit in 2009, has helped astronomers identify thousands of exoplanets, or planets outside our solar system. The discovery of exoplanets has helped astronomers understand that our solar system is just one of many that travels around the center of the Milky Way. Astronomers have even identified areas and exoplanets of the Milky Way that could have the right conditions to support life.

MY DISCOVERY

Search for the term *Milky Way* in an online search engine to learn more about our galaxy. What might happen to the solar system without the gravitational force exerted by the center of the galaxy?

The Milky Way is a spiral galaxy like the one shown here.

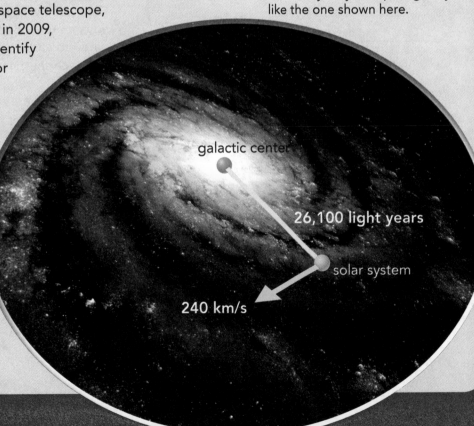

galactic center

26,100 light years

solar system

240 km/s

☑ TOPIC 2 Review and Assess

1 Solar System Objects

MS-ESS1-2, MS-ESS1-3

1. What characteristic do all the inner planets have in common?
   - **A.** ring system
   - **B.** liquid water
   - **C.** rocky surface
   - **D.** thick atmosphere

2. All the gas giants are surrounded by
   .... made up of small
   particles to very large chunks of ice and dust.

3. One astronomical unit is equal to the distance
   from .... to ....

4. **CCC Cause and Effect** Compare the conditions that led to the formation of the inner planets with those that led to the formation of the outer planets.

   ....
   ....
   ....
   ....
   ....
   ....
   ....
   ....
   ....
   ....
   ....
   ....
   ....
   ....
   ....
   ....
   ....
   ....

2 Learning About the Universe

MS-ESS1-3

5. Which object is the largest?
   - **A.** Earth
   - **B.** Saturn
   - **C.** Jupiter
   - **D.** the sun

6. A student is making a model of the sun's interior. Which feature should the student represent in the convection zone?
   - **A.** gas erupting into space
   - **B.** gases rising and sinking
   - **C.** radiation moving outward
   - **D.** nuclear fusion producing energy

7. Which technology makes it possible for people to live and work in space for long periods?
   - **A.** space probe
   - **B.** space station
   - **C.** radio telescope
   - **D.** optical telescope

8. **SEP Analyze Benefits** In 1981, the first space shuttle was launched from Cape Canaveral. Which statement describes an advantage that space shuttles have compared to earlier space probes and capsules?
   - **A.** Space shuttles can travel beyond Earth's orbit.
   - **B.** Space shuttles are inexpensive to build.
   - **C.** Space shuttles can be used more than once.
   - **D.** Space shuttles can travel beyond the solar system.

9. **Apply Concepts** Describe one kind of telescope and how you could use it to learn about an object in space.

   ....
   ....
   ....
   ....
   ....
   ....

10. Telescopes work by collecting and focusing different forms of ....
    radiation.

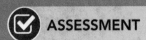
3 Stars

MS-ESS1-2

11. Using the H-R diagram, astronomers classify stars using which two star properties?
A. color and composition
B. size and surface temperature
C. surface temperature and absolute brightness
D. surface temperature and apparent brightness

12. Which property indicates a star's temperature?
A. size
B. color
C. composition
D. brightness

13. A .... forms when .... pulls together the gas and dust in the densest part of a nebula.

14. SEP Develop Models ✏ Draw a flow chart to model the stages in the life span of a high-mass star.

4 Galaxies

MS-ESS1-2

15. In what kind of star system does one star sometimes block the light from another?
A. open cluster
B. globular cluster
C. quasar system
D. eclipsing binary

16. What is the name of the explosion that began the universe?
A. solar nebula
B. big bang
C. dark matter
D. supernova

17. What is dark matter?
A. matter that can be seen directly
B. matter that does not give off electromagnetic radiation
C. matter that makes up about 10 percent of the mass of the universe
D. matter that has no effect on other objects

18. Compare and Contrast How do open clusters and globular clusters differ in terms of numbers of stars?

....

....

19. CCC Systems Determine the hierarchy of the universe in a list, starting with stars.

....

....

....

....

....

....

....

....

....

....

93

MS-ESS1-2

Evidence-Based Assessment

Willa is developing a model to help her study gravity. She wants to understand that role that gravity plays in keeping objects in the solar system in orbit around the sun. She plans on using some household materials to model a gravity well.

A gravity well is a representation of the gravitational field or pull of an object in space. A massive object like the sun has a deep gravity well. A less massive object, such as an asteroid, has a very shallow gravity well.

Willa stretches plastic wrap across a large hoop to represent the "fabric" of space. She has one large clay ball, some small marbles, and tiny ball bearings.

When Willa places the clay ball on the plastic, she observes that it sinks into the plastic and forms a well. When she places a marble or bearing near the ball, Willa observes the marble roll along the surface of the plastic toward the ball.

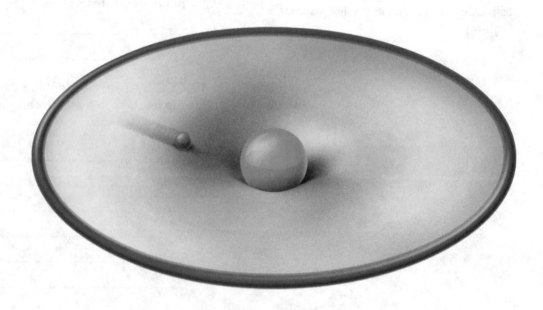

1. **SEP Develop Models** In Willa's model, which of the following solar system objects does the large clay ball represent?
   A. the sun
   B. a planet
   C. a moon
   D. an asteroid

2. **CCC System Models** Willa tests her model by placing the large clay ball, a single marble, and a single ball bearing one at at time on the plastic. Which object creates the deepest well? How can these observations be applied to solar system objects? Explain.

   ....

   ....

   ....

   ....

   ....

   ....

   ....

   ....

   ....

3. **SEP Identify Limitations** How does Willa's model show that gravity keeps objects in the solar system in orbit around the sun? What are the limitations of her model? Do objects in the solar system behave like they would in the model? Explain.

   ....

   ....

   ....

   ....

   ....

   ....

   ....

4. **SEP Construct Explanations** How can Willa use the materials and her model to explain why objects that are very far from the sun do not orbit it?

   ....

   ....

   ....

   ....

   ....

   ....

   ....

   ....

   ....

Quest FINDINGS

Complete the Quest!

Phenomenon You learned what it takes to be an asteroid hunter, an extraterrestrial life hunter, and a dark matter hunter. Apply the knowledge you gained to write advertisements to attract great candidates to the new observatory.

CCC Cause and Effect Think about the three different types of scientists needed. Why might it be important for them to use models in their investigations?

....

....

....

....

👆 **INTERACTIVITY**

Reflect on Searching for a Star

Scaling Down the Solar System

How can you **build scale models** of **volcanoes** from three **planets** to show which one is largest?

Background

Phenomenon Mauna Loa in Hawaii is currently the largest active volcano on Earth. But is it the largest volcano in the solar system? Sapas Mons on Venus and Olympus Mons on Mars are two other volcanoes that can be viewed from Earth with telescopes. Scientists use scale models to help them answer questions about landforms on other planets. In this investigation, you will make scale models of volcanoes found on different planets in our solar system.

Materials

(per group)

- calculator
- graph paper
- a variety of common craft materials, such as construction paper, tape, glue, craft sticks, modeling clay, foam, cotton balls, and markers
- metric ruler

Safety

Be sure to follow all safety guidelines provided by your teacher. The Safety Appendix of your textbook provides more details about the safety icons.

Mauna Loa, Hawaii

Sapas Mons

Olympus Mons

Procedure

HANDS-ON LAB

Demonstrate Go online for a downloadable worksheet of this lab.

☐ 1. Examine the images of the three volcanoes that are found on different planets in our solar system. Research the volcanoes to find out about their heights, diameters, and any other distinguishing characteristics. In the space provided on the next page, create a data table to record the names of the volcanoes, their locations, their heights (in km), and their diameters (in km).

☐ 2. Determine an appropriate scale for your models. This decision is affected by two factors: how big an area you need to model and how much detail you want to show. If you need to show a large area, then you would want to choose a smaller scale to avoid the model becoming too big. But at smaller scales, models are limited in the amount of detail they can show. Consider the details you want to show and how large or small you want the models to be. Take into account the greatest and smallest values in your data table. Choose a scale that will allow you to represent these values in the models appropriately.

Record the scale that you will use for your models.

1 km = _____

☐ 3. ✂ You will construct a three-dimensional model of each volcano from construction paper, modeling clay, or other available materials.

☐ 4. Draw a sketch to show your plans. Your sketch should indicate the scale of your models. It also should clearly identify the materials you will use in each part of your models. After obtaining your teacher's approval, follow your plan to construct your models to scale.

Data Table

Model Sketch

Analyze and Interpret Data

1. **SEP Construct Explanations** Could you have used a different scale for each volcano to represent their relative sizes? Explain.

   ....

   ....

2. **CCC Scale, Proportion, and Quantity** Suppose someone suggested that you add a scale model of a human to your volcano models. Is this a reasonable or unreasonable suggestion? Use the scale of the models to construct your answer. (*Note: The height of a typical adult human is slightly less than 2 m, or 0.002 km.*)

   ....

   ....

   ....

   ....

3. **SEP Use Models** When you are studying models of different solar system objects, how does identifying the scale of each model help you to compare and understand their sizes and features?

   ....

   ....

   ....

   ....

   ....

4. **Identify Limitations** Compare your models to the photographs of each volcano. What are some of the advantages of your models over the photographs? What are some of the disadvantages?

   ....

   ....

   ....

   ....

5. **SEP Evaluate Information** Using the scale models created by your class, compare characteristics such as the size and shape of the three different volcanoes found on Venus, Earth, and Mars. What can you infer about the three planets from this analysis?

   ....

   ....

   ....

SEP.1, SEP.8

The Meaning of Science

Science Skills

Reflect Think about a time you misplaced something and could not find it. Write a sentence defining the problem. What science skills could you use to solve the problem? Explain how you would use at least three of the skills in the table.

Science is a way of learning about the natural world. It involves asking questions, making predictions, and collecting information to see if the answer is right or wrong.

The table lists some of the skills that scientists use. You use some of these skills every day. For example, you may observe and evaluate your lunch options before choosing what to eat.

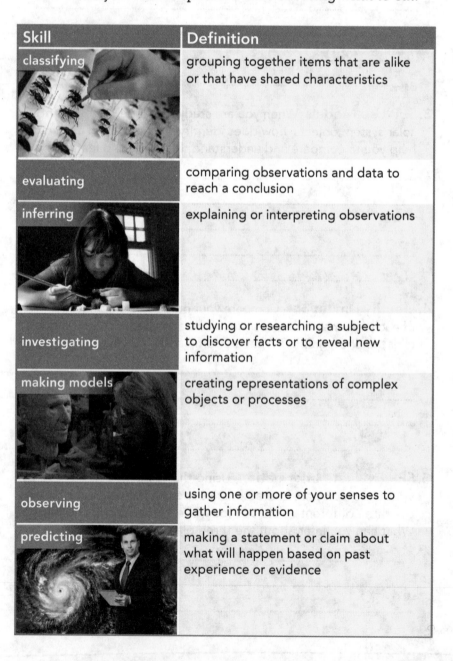

Skill	Definition
classifying	grouping together items that are alike or that have shared characteristics
evaluating	comparing observations and data to reach a conclusion
inferring	explaining or interpreting observations
investigating	studying or researching a subject to discover facts or to reveal new information
making models	creating representations of complex objects or processes
observing	using one or more of your senses to gather information
predicting	making a statement or claim about what will happen based on past experience or evidence

Scientific Attitudes

Curiosity often drives scientists to learn about the world around them. Creativity is useful for coming up with inventive ways to solve problems. Such qualities and attitudes, and the ability to keep an open mind, are essential for scientists.

When sharing results or findings, honesty and ethics are also essential. Ethics refers to rules for knowing right from wrong.

Being skeptical is also important. This means having doubts about things based on past experiences and evidence. Skepticism helps to prevent accepting data and results that may not be true.

Scientists must also avoid bias—likes or dislikes of people, ideas, or things. They must avoid experimental bias, which is a mistake that may make an experiment's preferred outcome more likely.

Scientific Reasoning

Scientific reasoning depends on being logical and objective. When you are objective, you use evidence and apply logic to draw conclusions. Being subjective means basing conclusions on personal feelings, biases, or opinions. Subjective reasoning can interfere with science and skew results. Objective reasoning helps scientists use observations to reach conclusions about the natural world.

Scientists use two types of objective reasoning: deductive and inductive. Deductive reasoning involves starting with a general idea or theory and applying it to a situation. For example, the theory of plate tectonics indicates that earthquakes happen mostly where tectonic plates meet. You could then draw the conclusion, or deduce, that California has many earthquakes because tectonic plates meet there.

In inductive reasoning, you make a generalization from a specific observation. When scientists collect data in an experiment and draw a conclusion based on that data, they use inductive reasoning. For example, if fertilizer causes one set of plants to grow faster than another, you might infer that the fertilizer promotes plant growth.

Make Meaning
Think about a bias the marine biologist in the photo could show that results in paying more or less attention to one kind of organism over others. Make a prediction about how that bias could affect the biologist's survey of the coral reef.

Write About It
Suppose it is raining when you go to sleep one night. When you wake up the next morning, you observe frozen puddles on the ground and icicles on tree branches. Use scientific reasoning to draw a conclusion about the air temperature outside. Support your conclusion using deductive or inductive reasoning.

SEP.1, SEP.2, SEP.3, SEP.4, CCC.4

Science Processes

Scientific Inquiry

Scientists contribute to scientific knowledge by conducting investigations and drawing conclusions. The process often begins with an observation that leads to a question, which is then followed by the development of a hypothesis. This is known as scientific inquiry.

One of the first steps in scientific inquiry is asking questions. However, it's important to make a question specific with a narrow focus so the investigation will not be too broad. A biologist may want to know all there is to know about wolves, for example. But a good, focused question for a specific inquiry might be "How many offspring does the average female wolf produce in her lifetime?"

A hypothesis is a possible answer to a scientific question. A hypothesis must be testable. For something to be testable, researchers must be able to carry out an investigation and gather evidence that will either support or disprove the hypothesis.

Scientific Models

Models are tools that scientists use to study phenomena indirectly. A model is any representation of an object or process. Illustrations, dioramas, globes, diagrams, computer programs, and mathematical equations are all examples of scientific models. For example, a diagram of Earth's crust and mantle can help you to picture layers deep below the surface and understand events such as volcanic eruptions.

Models also allow scientists to represent objects that are either very large, such as our solar system, or very small, such as a molecule of DNA. Models can also represent processes that occur over a long period of time, such as the changes that have occurred throughout Earth's history.

Models are helpful, but they have limitations. Physical models are not made of the same materials as the objects they represent. Most models of complex objects or processes show only major parts, stages, or relationships. Many details are left out. Therefore, you may not be able to learn as much from models as you would through direct observation.

Science Experiments

An experiment or investigation must be well planned to produce valid results. In planning an experiment, you must identify the independent and dependent variables. You must also do as much as possible to remove the effects of other variables. A controlled experiment is one in which you test only one variable at a time.

For example, suppose you plan a controlled experiment to learn how the type of material affects the speed at which sound waves travel through it. The only variable that should change is the type of material. This way, if the speed of sound changes, you know that it is a result of a change in the material, not another variable such as the thickness of the material or the type of sound used.

You should also remove bias from any investigation. You may inadvertently introduce bias by selecting subjects you like and avoiding those you don't like. Scientists often conduct investigations by taking random samples to avoid ending up with biased results.

Once you plan your investigation and begin to collect data, it's important to record and organize the data. You may wish to use a graph to display and help you to interpret the data.

Communicating is the sharing of ideas and results with others through writing and speaking. Communicating data and conclusions is a central part of science.

Scientists share knowledge, including new findings, theories, and techniques for collecting data. Conferences, journals, and websites help scientists to communicate with each other. Popular media, including newspapers, magazines, and social media sites, help scientists to share their knowledge with nonscientists. However, before the results of investigations are shared and published, other scientists should review the experiment for possible sources of error, such as bias and unsupported conclusions.

Write About It

List four ways you could communicate the results of a scientific study about the health of sea turtles in the Pacific Ocean.

SEP.1, SEP.6, SEP.7, SEP.8

Scientific Knowledge

Scientific Explanations

Suppose you learn that adult flamingos are pink because of the food they eat. This statement is a scientific explanation—it describes how something in nature works or explains why it happens. Scientists from different fields use methods such as researching information, designing experiments, and making models to form scientific explanations. Scientific explanations often result from many years of work and multiple investigations conducted by many scientists.

Scientific Theories and Laws

A scientific law is a statement that describes what you can expect to occur every time under a particular set of conditions. A scientific law describes an observed pattern in nature, but it does not attempt to explain it. For example, the law of superposition describes what you can expect to find in terms of the ages of layers of rock. Geologists use this observed pattern to determine the relative ages of sedimentary rock layers. But the law does not explain why the pattern occurs.

By contrast, a scientific theory is a well-tested explanation for a wide range of observations or experimental results. It provides details and describes causes of observed patterns. Something is elevated to a theory only when there is a large body of evidence that supports it. However, a scientific theory can be changed or overturned when new evidence is found.

📓 Write About It
Choose two fields of science that interest you. Describe a method used to develop scientific explanations in each field.

SEP Construct Explanations Complete the table to compare and contrast a scientific theory and a scientific law.

	Scientific Theory	Scientific Law
Definition		
Does it attempt to explain a pattern observed in nature?		

Analyzing Scientific Explanations

To analyze scientific explanations that you hear on the news or read in a book such as this one, you need scientific literacy. Scientific literacy means understanding scientific terms and principles well enough to ask questions, evaluate information, and make decisions. Scientific reasoning gives you a process to apply. This includes looking for bias and errors in the research, evaluating data, and identifying faulty reasoning. For example, by evaluating how a survey was conducted, you may find a serious flaw in the researchers' methods.

Evidence and Opinions

The basis for scientific explanations is empirical evidence. Empirical evidence includes the data and observations that have been collected through scientific processes. Satellite images, photos, and maps of mountains and volcanoes are all examples of empirical evidence that support a scientific explanation about Earth's tectonic plates. Scientists look for patterns when they analyze this evidence. For example, they might see a pattern that mountains and volcanoes often occur near tectonic plate boundaries.

To evaluate scientific information, you must first distinguish between evidence and opinion. In science, evidence includes objective observations and conclusions that have been repeated. Evidence may or may not support a scientific claim. An opinion is a subjective idea that is formed from evidence, but it cannot be confirmed by evidence.

Write About It
Suppose the conservation committee of a town wants to gauge residents' opinions about a proposal to stock the local ponds with fish every spring. The committee pays for a survey to appear on a web site that is popular with people who like to fish. The results of the survey show 78 people in favor of the proposal and two against it. Do you think the survey's results are valid? Explain.

Make Meaning
Explain what empirical evidence the photograph reveals.

SEP.3, SEP.4

Tools of Science

Measurement

Making measurements using standard units is important in all fields of science. This allows scientists to repeat and reproduce other experiments, as well as to understand the precise meaning of the results of others. Scientists use a measurement system called the International System of Units, or SI.

For each type of measurement, there is a series of units that are greater or less than each other. The unit a scientist uses depends on what is being measured. For example, a geophysicist tracking the movements of tectonic plates may use centimeters, as plates tend to move small amounts each year. Meanwhile, a marine biologist might measure the movement of migrating bluefin tuna on the scale of kilometers.

Units for length, mass, volume, and density are based on powers of ten—a meter is equal to 100 centimeters or 1000 millimeters. Units of time do not follow that pattern. There are 60 seconds in a minute, 60 minutes in an hour, and 24 hours in a day. These units are based on patterns that humans perceived in nature. Units of temperature are based on scales that are set according to observations of nature. For example, 0°C is the temperature at which pure water freezes, and 100°C is the temperature at which it boils.

Write About It
Suppose you are planning an investigation in which you must measure the dimensions of several small mineral samples that fit in your hand. Which metric unit or units will you most likely use? Explain your answer.

Measurement	Metric units
Length or distance	meter (m), kilometer (km), centimeter (cm), millimeter (mm) 1 km = 1,000 m 1 cm = 10 mm 1 m = 100 cm
Mass	kilogram (kg), gram (g), milligram (mg) 1 kg = 1,000 g 1 g = 1,000 mg
Volume	cubic meter (m^3), cubic centimeter (cm^3) 1 m^3 = 1,000,000 cm^3
Density	kilogram per cubic meter (kg/m^3), gram per cubic centimeter (g/cm^3) 1,000 kg/m^3 = 1 g/cm^3
Temperature	degrees Celsius (°C), kelvin (K) 1°C = 273 K
Time	hour (h), minute (m), second (s)

Math Skills

Using numbers to collect and interpret data involves math skills that are essential in science. For example, you use math skills when you estimate the number of birds in an entire forest after counting the actual number of birds in ten trees.

Scientists evaluate measurements and estimates for their precision and accuracy. In science, an accurate measurement is very close to the actual value. Precise measurements are very close, or nearly equal, to each other. Reliable measurements are both accurate and precise. An imprecise value may be a sign of an error in data collection. This kind of anomalous data may be excluded to avoid skewing the data and harming the investigation.

Other math skills include performing specific calculations, such as finding the mean, or average, value in a data set. The mean can be calculated by adding up all of the values in the data set and then dividing that sum by the number of values.

Hour	Number of Ducks Observed at a Pond
1	12
2	10
3	2
4	14
5	13
6	10
7	11

SEP Use Mathematics The data table shows how many ducks were seen at a pond every hour over the course of seven hours. Is there a data point that seems anomalous? If so, cross out that data point. Then, calculate the mean number of ducks on the pond. Round the mean to the nearest whole number.

Graphs

Graphs help scientists to interpret data by helping them to find trends or patterns in the data. A line graph displays data that show how one variable (the dependent or outcome variable) changes in response to another (the independent or test variable). The slope and shape of a graph line can reveal patterns and help scientists to make predictions. For example, line graphs can help you to spot patterns of change over time.

Scientists use bar graphs to compare data across categories or subjects that may not affect each other. The heights of the bars make it easy to compare those quantities. A circle graph, also known as a pie chart, shows the proportions of different parts of a whole.

Write About It
You and a friend record the distance you travel every 15 minutes on a one-hour bike trip. Your friend wants to display the data as a circle graph. Explain whether or not this is the best type of graph to display your data. If not, suggest another graph to use.

SEP.1, SEP.2, SEP.3, SEP.6

The Engineering Design Process

Engineers are builders and problem solvers. Chemical engineers experiment with new fuels made from algae. Civil engineers design roadways and bridges. Bioengineers develop medical devices and prosthetics. The common trait among engineers is an ability to identify problems and design solutions to solve them. Engineers use a creative process that relies on scientific methods to help guide them from a concept or idea all the way to the final product.

Define the Problem

To identify or define a problem, different questions need to be asked: *What are the effects of the problem? What are the likely causes? What other factors could be involved?* Sometimes the obvious, immediate cause of a problem may be the result of another problem that may not be immediately apparent. For example, climate change results in different weather patterns, which in turn can affect organisms that live in certain habitats. So engineers must be aware of all the possible effects of potential solutions. Engineers must also take into account how well different solutions deal with the different causes of the problem.

Reflect Write about a problem that you encountered in your life that had both immediate, obvious causes as well as less-obvious and less-immediate ones.

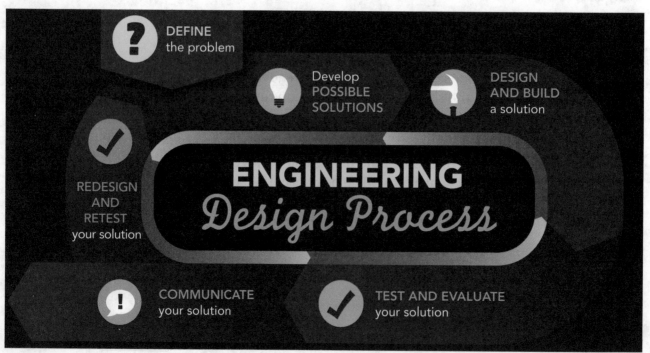

DEFINE the problem

Develop **POSSIBLE SOLUTIONS**

DESIGN AND BUILD a solution

REDESIGN AND RETEST your solution

ENGINEERING *Design Process*

COMMUNICATE your solution

TEST AND EVALUATE your solution

As engineers consider problems and design solutions, they must identify and categorize the criteria and constraints of the project.

Criteria are the factors that must be met or accomplished by the solution. For example, a gardener who wants to protect outdoor plants from deer and rabbits may say that the criteria for the solution are "plants are no longer eaten" and "plant growth is not inhibited in any way." The gardener then knows the plants cannot simply be sealed off from the environment, because the plants will not receive sunlight and water.

The same gardener will likely have constraints on his solution, such as budget for materials and time that is available for working on the project. By setting constraints, a solution can be designed that will be successful without introducing a new set of problems. No one wants to spend $500 on materials to protect $100 worth of tomatoes and cucumbers.

Develop Possible Solutions

After the problem has been identified, and the criteria and constraints identified, an engineer will consider possible solutions. This often involves working in teams with other engineers and designers to brainstorm ideas and research materials that can be used in the design.

It's important for engineers to think creatively and explore all potential solutions. If you wanted to design a bicycle that was safer and easier to ride than a traditional bicycle, then you would want more than just one or two solutions. Having multiple ideas to choose from increases the likelihood that you will develop a solution that meets the criteria and constraints. In addition, different ideas that result from brainstorming can often lead to new and better solutions to an existing problem.

Make Meaning
Using the example of a garden that is vulnerable to wild animals such as deer, make a list of likely constraints on an engineering solution to the problem you identified before. Determine if there are common traits among the constraints, and identify categories for them.

Design a Solution

Engineers then develop the idea that they feel best solves the problem. Once a solution has been chosen, engineers and designers get to work building a model or prototype of the solution. A model may involve sketching on paper or using computer software to construct a model of the solution. A prototype is a working model of the solution.

Building a model or prototype helps an engineer determine whether a solution meets the criteria and stays within the constraints. During this stage of the process, engineers must often deal with new problems and make any necessary adjustments to the model or prototype.

Test and Evaluate a Solution

Make Meaning Think about an aluminum beverage can. What would happen if the price or availability of aluminum changed so much that cans needed to be made of a new material? What would the criteria and constraints be on the development of a new can?

Whether testing a model or a prototype, engineers use scientific processes to evaluate their solutions. Multiple experiments, tests, or trials are conducted, data are evaluated, and results and analyses are communicated. New criteria or constraints may emerge as a result of testing. In most cases, a solution will require some refinement or revision, even if it has been through successful testing. Refining a solution is necessary if there are new constraints, such as less money or available materials. Additional testing may be done to ensure that a solution satisfies local, state, or federal laws or standards.

A naval architect sets up a model to test how the the hull's design responds to waves.

Communicate the Solution

Engineers need to communicate the final design to the people who will manufacture the product. This may include sketches, detailed drawings, computer simulations, and written text. Engineers often provide evidence that was collected during the testing stage. This evidence may include graphs and data tables that support the decisions made for the final design.

If there is feedback about the solution, then the engineers and designers must further refine the solution. This might involve making minor adjustments to the design, or it might mean bigger modifications to the design based on new criteria or constraints. Any changes in the design will require additional testing to make sure that the changes work as intended.

Redesign and Retest the Solution

At different steps in the engineering and design process, a solution usually must be revised and retested. Many designs fail to work perfectly, even after models and prototypes are built, tested, and evaluated. Engineers must be ready to analyze new results and deal with any new problems that arise. Troubleshooting, or fixing design problems, allows engineers to adjust the design to improve on how well the solution meets the need.

SEP Communicate Information Suppose you are an engineer at an aerospace company. Your team is designing a rover to be used on a future NASA space mission. A family member doesn't understand why so much of your team's time is taken up with testing and retesting the rover design. What are three things you would tell your relative to explain why testing and retesting are so important to the engineering and design process?

....

....

....

....

....

....

....

....

APPENDIX A

Safety Symbols

These symbols warn of possible dangers in the laboratory and remind you to work carefully.

 Safety Goggles Wear safety goggles to protect your eyes in any activity involving chemicals, flames or heating, or glassware.

 Lab Apron Wear a laboratory apron to protect your skin and clothing from damage.

 Breakage Handle breakable materials, such as glassware, with care. Do not touch broken glassware.

 Heat-Resistant Gloves Use an oven mitt or other hand protection when handling hot materials, such as hot plates or hot glassware.

 Plastic Gloves Wear disposable plastic gloves when working with harmful chemicals and organisms. Keep your hands away from your face, and dispose of the gloves according to your teacher's instructions.

 Heating Use a clamp or tongs to pick up hot glassware. Do not touch hot objects with your bare hands.

 Flames Before you work with flames, tie back loose hair and clothing. Follow your teacher's instructions about lighting and extinguishing flames.

 No Flames When using flammable materials, make sure there are no flames, sparks, or other exposed heat sources present.

 Corrosive Chemical Avoid getting acid or other corrosive chemicals on your skin or clothing or in your eyes. Do not inhale the vapors. Wash your hands after the activity.

 Poison Do not let any poisonous chemical come into contact with your skin, and do not inhale its vapors. Wash your hands when you are finished with the activity.

 Fumes Work in a well-ventilated area when harmful vapors may be involved. Avoid inhaling vapors directly. Test an odor only when directed to do so by your teacher, and use a wafting motion to direct the vapor toward your nose.

 Sharp Object Scissors, scalpels, knives, needles, pins, and tacks can cut your skin. Always direct a sharp edge or point away from yourself and others.

 Animal Safety Treat live or preserved animals or animal parts with care to avoid harming the animals or yourself. Wash your hands when you are finished with the activity.

 Plant Safety Handle plants only as directed by your teacher. If you are allergic to certain plants, tell your teacher; do not do an activity involving those plants. Avoid touching harmful plants such as poison ivy. Wash your hands when you are finished with the activity.

 Electric Shock To avoid electric shock, never use electrical equipment around water, when the equipment is wet, or when your hands are wet. Be sure cords are untangled and cannot trip anyone. Unplug equipment not in use.

 Physical Safety When an experiment involves physical activity, avoid injuring yourself or others. Alert your teacher if there is any reason you should not participate.

 Disposal Dispose of chemicals and other laboratory materials safely. Follow the instructions from your teacher.

 Hand Washing Wash your hands thoroughly when finished with an activity. Use soap and warm water. Rinse well.

 General Safety Awareness When this symbol appears, follow the instructions provided. When you are asked to develop your own procedure in a lab, have your teacher approve your plan.

Using a Laboratory Balance

The laboratory balance is an important tool in scientific investigations. Different kinds of balances are used in the laboratory to determine the masses and weights of objects. You can use a triple-beam balance to determine the masses of materials that you study or experiment with in the laboratory. An electronic balance, unlike a triple-beam balance, is used to measure the weights of materials.

The triple-beam balance that you may use in your science class is probably similar to the balance depicted in this Appendix. To use the balance properly, you should learn the name, location, and function of each part of the balance.

Triple-Beam Balance

The triple-beam balance is a single-pan balance with three beams calibrated in grams. The back, or 100-gram, beam is divided into ten units of 10 grams each. The middle, or 500-gram, beam is divided into five units of 100 grams each. The front, or 10-gram, beam is divided into ten units of 1 gram each. Each gram on the front beam is further divided into units of 0.1 gram.

Apply Concepts What is the greatest mass you could find with the triple-beam balance in the picture?

....

Calculate What is the mass of the apple in the picture?

....

The following procedure can be used to find the mass of an object with a triple-beam balance:

1. Place the object on the pan.
2. Move the rider on the middle beam notch by notch until the horizontal pointer on the right drops below zero. Move the rider back one notch.
3. Move the rider on the back beam notch by notch until the pointer again drops below zero. Move the rider back one notch.
4. Slowly slide the rider along the front beam until the pointer stops at the zero point.
5. The mass of the object is equal to the sum of the readings on the three beams.

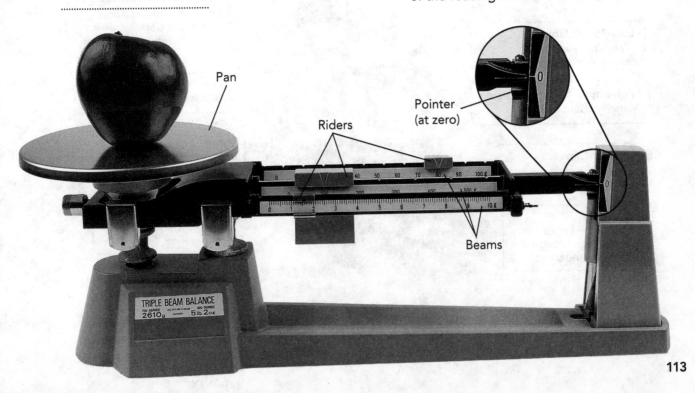

Pan

Riders

Pointer (at zero)

Beams

TRIPLE BEAM BALANCE
2610g   5lb 2oz

Using a Microscope

The microscope is an essential tool in the study of life science. It allows you to see things that are too small to be seen with the unaided eye.

You will probably use a compound microscope like the one you see here. The compound microscope has more than one lens that magnifies the object you view.

Typically, a compound microscope has one lens in the eyepiece (the part you look through). The eyepiece lens usually magnifies 10×. Any object you view through this lens will appear 10 times larger than it is.

A compound microscope may contain two or three other lenses called objective lenses. They are called the low-power and high-power objective lenses. The low-power objective lens usually magnifies 10×. The high-power objective lenses usually magnify 40× and 100×.

To calculate the total magnification with which you are viewing an object, multiply the magnification of the eyepiece lens by the magnification of the objective lens you are using. For example, the eyepiece's magnification of 10× multiplied by the low-power objective's magnification of 10× equals a total magnification of 100×.

Use the photo of the compound microscope to become familiar with the parts of the microscope and their functions.

The Parts of a Microscope

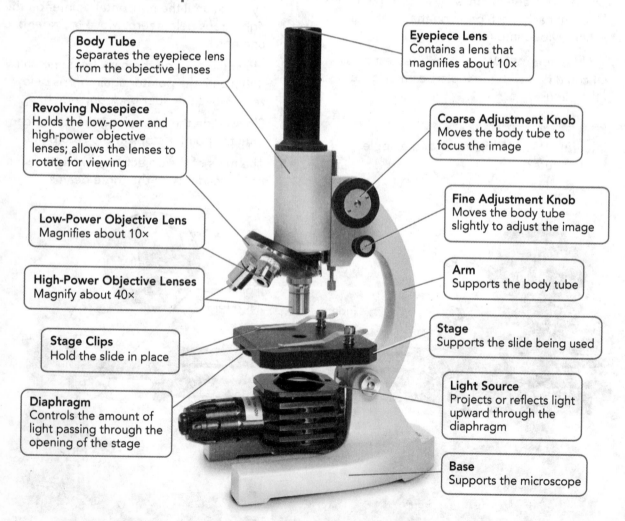

Body Tube
Separates the eyepiece lens from the objective lenses

Revolving Nosepiece
Holds the low-power and high-power objective lenses; allows the lenses to rotate for viewing

Low-Power Objective Lens
Magnifies about 10×

High-Power Objective Lenses
Magnify about 40×

Stage Clips
Hold the slide in place

Diaphragm
Controls the amount of light passing through the opening of the stage

Eyepiece Lens
Contains a lens that magnifies about 10×

Coarse Adjustment Knob
Moves the body tube to focus the image

Fine Adjustment Knob
Moves the body tube slightly to adjust the image

Arm
Supports the body tube

Stage
Supports the slide being used

Light Source
Projects or reflects light upward through the diaphragm

Base
Supports the microscope

Using the Microscope
Use the following procedures when you are working with a microscope.

1. To carry the microscope, grasp the microscope's arm with one hand. Place your other hand under the base.

2. Place the microscope on a table with the arm toward you.

3. Turn the coarse adjustment knob to raise the body tube.

4. Revolve the nosepiece until the low-power objective lens clicks into place.

5. Adjust the diaphragm. While looking through the eyepiece, adjust the mirror until you see a bright white circle of light. **CAUTION:** Never use direct sunlight as a light source.

6. Place a slide on the stage. Center the specimen over the opening on the stage. Use the stage clips to hold the slide in place. **CAUTION:** Glass slides are fragile.

7. Look at the stage from the side. Carefully turn the coarse adjustment knob to lower the body tube until the low-power objective almost touches the slide.

8. Looking through the eyepiece, very slowly turn the coarse adjustment knob until the specimen comes into focus.

9. To switch to the high-power objective lens, look at the microscope from the side. Carefully revolve the nosepiece until the high-power objective lens clicks into place. Make sure the lens does not hit the slide.

10. Looking through the eyepiece, turn the fine adjustment knob until the specimen comes into focus.

Making a Wet-Mount Slide
Use the following procedures to make a wet-mount slide of a specimen.

1. Obtain a clean microscope slide and a coverslip. **CAUTION:** Glass slides and coverslips are fragile.

2. Place the specimen on the center of the slide. The specimen must be thin enough for light to pass through it.

3. Using a plastic dropper, place a drop of water on the specimen.

4. Gently place one edge of the coverslip against the slide so that it touches the edge of the water drop at a 45° angle. Slowly lower the coverslip over the specimen. If you see air bubbles trapped beneath the coverslip, tap the coverslip gently with the eraser end of a pencil.

5. Remove any excess water at the edge of the coverslip with a paper towel.

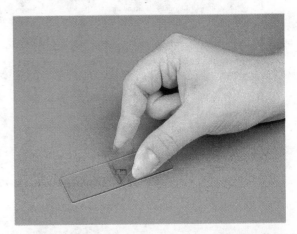

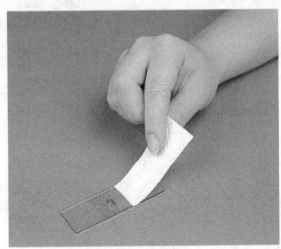

Periodic Table of Elements

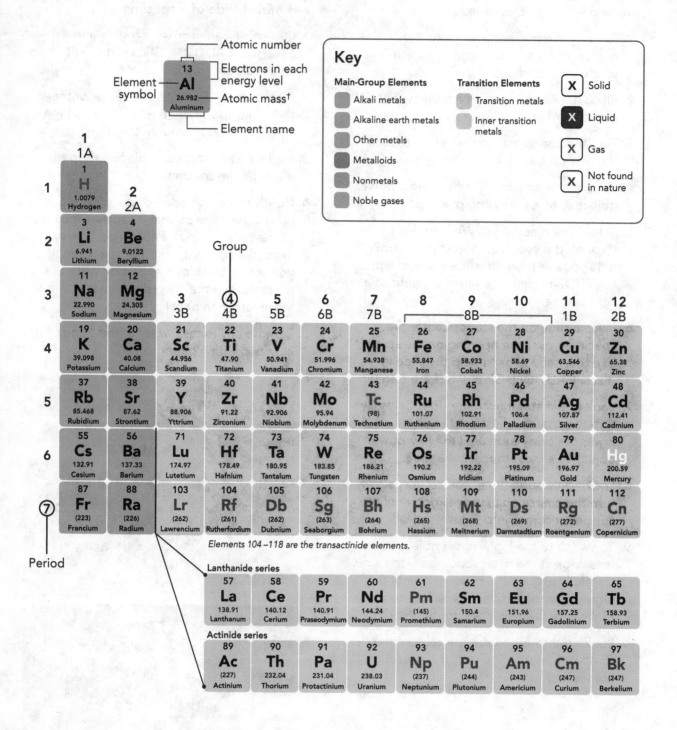

Elements 104–118 are the transactinide elements.

†The atomic masses in parentheses are the mass numbers of the longest-lived isotope of elements for which a standard atomic mass cannot be defined.

18 8A
2 **He** 4.0026 Helium

13 3A	14 4A	15 5A	16 6A	17 7A	
5 **B** 10.81 Boron	6 **C** 12.011 Carbon	7 **N** 14.007 Nitrogen	8 **O** 15.999 Oxygen	9 **F** 18.998 Fluorine	10 **Ne** 20.179 Neon
13 **Al** 26.982 Aluminum	14 **Si** 28.086 Silicon	15 **P** 30.974 Phosphorus	16 **S** 32.06 Sulfur	17 **Cl** 35.453 Chlorine	18 **Ar** 39.948 Argon
31 **Ga** 69.72 Gallium	32 **Ge** 72.59 Germanium	33 **As** 74.922 Arsenic	34 **Se** 78.96 Selenium	35 **Br** 79.904 Bromine	36 **Kr** 83.80 Krypton
49 **In** 114.82 Indium	50 **Sn** 118.69 Tin	51 **Sb** 121.75 Antimony	52 **Te** 127.60 Tellurium	53 **I** 126.90 Iodine	54 **Xe** 131.30 Xenon
81 **Tl** 204.37 Thallium	82 **Pb** 207.2 Lead	83 **Bi** 208.98 Bismuth	84 **Po** (209) Polonium	85 **At** (210) Astatine	86 **Rn** (222) Radon
113 **Nh** (284) Nihonium	114 **Fl** (289) Flerovium	115 **Mc** (288) Moscovium	116 **Lv** (292) Livermorium	117 **Ts** (294) Tennessine	118 **Og** (294) Oganesson

66 **Dy** 162.50 Dysprosium	67 **Ho** 164.93 Holmium	68 **Er** 167.26 Erbium	69 **Tm** 168.93 Thulium	70 **Yb** 173.04 Ytterbium
98 **Cf** (251) Californium	99 **Es** (252) Einsteinium	100 **Fm** (257) Fermium	101 **Md** (258) Mendelevium	102 **No** (259) Nobelium

GLOSSARY

A

absolute brightness The brightness a star would have if it were at a standard distance from Earth. (79)

apparent brightness The brightness of a star as seen from Earth. (79)

asteroid One of the rocky objects revolving around the sun that is too small and numerous to be considered a planet. (52)

astronomical unit A unit of distance equal to the average distance between Earth and the sun, about 150 million kilometers. (50)

axis An imaginary line that passes through a planet's center and its north and south poles, about which the planet rotates. (17)

B

big bang The initial explosion that resulted in the formation and expansion of the universe. (88)

C

comet A loose collection of ice and dust that orbits the sun, typically in a long, narrow orbit. (6, 52)

constellation A pattern or grouping of stars that people imagine to represent a figure or object. (7)

E

eclipse The partial or total blocking of one object in space by another. (31)

electromagnetic radiation The energy transferred through space by electromagnetic waves. (63)

ellipse An oval shape, which may be elongated or nearly circular; the shape of the planets' orbits. (11)

equinox Either of the two days of the year on which neither hemisphere is tilted toward or away from the sun. (20)

G

galaxy A huge group of single stars, star systems, star clusters, dust, and gas bound together by gravity. (85)

geocentric Term describing a model of the universe in which Earth is at the center of the revolving planets and stars. (10)

gravity The attractive force between objects; the force that moves objects downhill. (21)

H

heliocentric Term describing a model of the solar system in which Earth and the other planets revolve around the sun. (11)

I

inertia The tendency of an object to resist a change in motion. (22)

L

law of universal gravitation The scientific law that states that every object in the universe attracts every other object. (21)

light-year The distance that light travels in one year, about 9.46 trillion kilometers. (86)

M

meteor A streak of light in the sky produced by the burning of a meteoroid in Earth's atmosphere. (6)

meteoroid A chunk of rock or dust in space, generally smaller than an asteroid. (52)

moon A natural satellite that orbits a planet. (52)

N

neap tide The tide with the least difference between consecutive low and high tides. (33)

nebula A large cloud of gas and dust in space. (73)

O

orbit The path of an object as it revolves around another object in space. (18)

P

penumbra The part of a shadow surrounding the darkest part. (31)

phase One of the different apparent shapes of the moon as seen from Earth. (27)

planet An object that orbits a star, is large enough to have become rounded by its own gravity, and has cleared the area of its orbit. (5, 51)

protostar A contracting cloud of gas and dust with enough mass to form a star. (73)

R

revolution The movement of an object around another object. (18)

rotation The spinning motion of a planet on its axis. (17)

S

satellite An object that orbits a planet. (5)

solar system The system consisting of the sun and the planets and other objects that revolve around it. (49)

solstice Either of the two days of the year on which the sun reaches its greatest distance north or south of the equator. (20)

spectrum The range of wavelengths of electromagnetic waves. (63)

spring tide The tide with the greatest difference between consecutive low and high tides. (33)

star A ball of hot gas, primarily hydrogen and helium, that undergoes nuclear fusion. (5)

sun A large, gaseous body at the center of the solar system. (51)

supernova The brilliant explosion of a dying supergiant star. (75)

T

telescope An optical instrument that forms enlarged images of distant objects. (64)

tide The periodic rise and fall of the level of water in the ocean. (32)

U

umbra The darkest part of a shadow. (31)

universe All of space and everything in it. (86)

V

visible light Electromagnetic radiation that can be seen with the unaided eye. (63)

W

wavelength The distance between two corresponding parts of a wave, such as the distance between two crests. (63)

white dwarf The blue-white hot core of a star that is left behind after its outer layers have expanded and drifted out into space. (75)

INDEX

Page numbers for key terms are printed in boldface type.

CREDITS

Photographs
Photo locators denoted as follows: Top (T), Center (C), Bottom (B), Left (L), Right (R), Background (Bkgd)

Covers
Front Cover: Tim Kopra/NASA
Back Cover: LHF Graphics/Shutterstock

Front Matter
iv: Clari Massimiliano/Shutterstock; vi: Chris Cook/Science Source; vii: John A. Davis/Shutterstock; viii: Brian J. Skerry/National Geographic/Getty Images; ix: Gary Meszaros/Science Source/Getty Images.

Topic 1
x: Chris Cook/Science Source;002: Paul Lindsay/Alamy Stock Photo; 004: Scott Stulberg/Getty Images; 006: Halley Multicolor Camera Team, Giotto Project, ESA; 008: Alan Dyer/VWPics/Alamy Stock Photo; 014: AF Fotografie/Alamy Stock Photo; 016: Triff /NASA/Shutterstock; 020: David Clapp/Shutterstock; 021: NASA/Getty Images; 025 Bkgrd: EFesenko/Shutterstock; 025 CR: IStock/Getty Images; 026: David M. Schrader/Shutterstock; 028: Quaoar/Shutterstock; 030 BL: Chris Collins/Shutterstock; 030 CL: Oorka/Shutterstock; 040: Quaoar/Shutterstock; 041: Claudio Divizia/Shutterstock;

Topic 2
046: Blickwinkel/Alamy Stock Photo; 047 B: Ivann/Shutterstock; 047 CL: Robert_S/Shutterstock; 052 TL: John A. Davis/Shutterstock; 052 TL: JPL/NASA; 052 TR: NASA/Shutterstock; 055 TL: NASA; 055 TR: Ivann/Shutterstock; 060 BL: JPL Caltech/UMD/NASA; 060 CL: JPL Caltech/UCAL/MPS/DLR/IDA/NASA; 060 L: NASA; 060 TL: NASA; 064:

Hubble & NASA/S. Smartt/ESA/NASA; 066: European Space Agency; 067: Comstock Images/Getty Images; 068 BR: NASA; 068 CR: Sovfoto/UIG/Getty Images; 068 TR: Sovfoto/UIG/Getty Images; 069 BC: John Baran/Alamy Stock Photo; 069 TR: NASA; 070 BL: NASA & ESA; 070 CL: Everett Historical/Shutterstock; 070 TR: Stocktrek Images, Inc./Alamy Stock Photo; 071 BL: JPL/NASA; 071 CR: Tim Jacobs/NASA; 071 TL: NASA; 076: Peresanz/Shutterstock; 079: NASA/S.Dupuis/Alamy Stock Photo; 083: Igordabari/Shutterstock; 086: G. Illingworth, D. Magee, and P. Oesch, University of California, Santa Cruz; R. Bouwens, Leiden University; and the HUDF09 Team/ESA/NASA; 090: Albert Barr/Shutterstock; 095: NASA; 096: Dhoxax/Getty Images; 097 TL: JPL/NASA; 097 TR: Stocktrek Images/Getty Images;

End Matter
100 BCL: Philippe Plailly & Elisabeth Daynes/Science Source; 100 BL: EHStockphoto/Shutterstock; 100 TCL: Cyndi Monaghan/Getty Images; 100 TL: Javier Larrea/AGE Fotostock; 101: WaterFrame/Alamy Stock Photo; 102: Africa Studio/Shutterstock; 103: Jeff Rotman/Alamy Stock Photo; 104: Grant Faint/Getty Images; 105: Ross Armstrong/Alamy Stock Photo; 106: Geoz/Alamy Stock Photo; 109: Martin Shields/Alamy Stock Photo; 110: Nicola Tree/Getty Images; 111: Regan Geeseman/NASA; 113: Pearson Education Ltd.; 114: Pearson Education Ltd.; 115 BR: Pearson Education Ltd.; 115 TR: Pearson Education Ltd.

Program graphics: ArtMari/Shutterstock; BeatWalk/Shutterstock; Irmun/Shutterstock; LHF Graphics/Shutterstock; Multigon/Shutterstock; Nikolaeva/Shutterstock; silm/Shutterstock; Undrey/Shutterstock

Take Notes

Use this space for recording notes and sketching out ideas.

Take Notes

Use this space for recording notes and sketching out ideas.

Take Notes